DUNCAN L

AUTOMATICS

FAST FIREPOWER, TACTICAL SUPERIORITY

DUNCAN LONG

AUTOMATICS
FAST FIREPOWER, TACTICAL SUPERIORITY

PALADIN PRESS
BOULDER, COLORADO

Automatics: Fast Firepower, Tactical Superiority
by Duncan Long
Copyright © 1986 by Duncan Long

ISBN 0-87364-397-6
Printed in the United States of America

Published by Paladin Press, a division of
Paladin Enterprises, Inc., P.O. Box 1307,
Boulder, Colorado 80306, USA.
(303) 443-7250

Direct inquiries and/or orders to the above address.

Front cover photos courtesy of Browning, Colt Firearms, Glock, Inc.,
Raven Arms, and Sturm, Ruger & Company, Inc.

Back cover photos courtesy of Arminex, Iver Johnson, L.A.R.
Manufacturing, Smith & Wesson, and Sturm, Ruger & Company, Inc.

Contents

Warning

Technical data presented here, particularly on ammunition and the use, adjustment, and alteration of firearms, inevitably reflects the author's individual beliefs and experience with particular firearms, equipment, and components under specific circumstances which the reader cannot duplicate. The information in this book should therefore be used for guidance only and approached with great caution. Neither the author nor the publisher assume any responsibility for the use or misuse of information contained in this book.

Acknowledgments

Thanks must go to Charter Arms, Jennings, Beretta, Heckler & Koch, Colt, Raven Arms, Arminex, and Sturm, Ruger which so graciously loaned or gave me firearms to test out during the writing of this book and to the many, many companies which sent sample firearms accessories and products to inspect. Thanks must also go to Omark Industries (CCI and Speer), Norma, Hodgdon, Hercules, Federal Cartridge Corporation, Olin (Winchester), and Lee Precision, Inc., all of which helped keep me "in ammunition" to test out the weapons covered in this book. Too, thanks must go to the fine people at Paladin Press for their ideas and encouragement as well as making this book possible.

Thanks to my dad for his work in processing photos and to Don Riffey for his advice and use of his firearms. And of course my "usual" special thanks to Maggie, Kristen, and Nicholas.

Introduction

There's not enough space to start with the basics in a book like this. If you're interested in guns but know next to nothing about them, a quick trip to your local library or gun store should help you find some books on the subject. Likewise, this book will not look at the use of pistols for hunting, target practice, or combat games. As technology and techniques are refined, the gap between combat weapons and sporting guns is ever widening. One gun can serve many purposes, but multiple use will become less and less appropriate as time goes on.

I assume that you know which end of the gun is the muzzle; know a few of the basic parts like the extractor, hammer, etc.; have some idea of how firearms work; and know how to handle a firearm safely. If not, you should get help from someone who does. Trying to use a firearm without proper knowledge and safety practices is a good way to have an accident and perhaps even kill someone.

Traditionally, a pistol was any hand-held firearm other than a revolver. Derringers, automatics, single-shot handguns, and even sawed-off rifles and shotguns could all technically be "pistols," but a revolver was a revolver. How this ever got started

is hard to say. Samuel Colt, inventor of the first practical revolver, used the word "pistol" to describe his repeating firearms. Only later did Colt Patent Fire Arms Manufacturing Company use the word "revolver" to describe Samuel Colt's invention. Currently, common usage is starting to catch up with Samuel Colt and most of us have come to toss revolvers into the "pistol" pot.

Another potentially confusing term is the "automatic." An automatic pistol is one that reloads itself from a magazine after a shot is fired. Such guns reload automatically rather than firing automatically like a submachine gun. So an "automatic" pistol is actually a "semiautomatic" firearm; one squeeze of the trigger only fires one shot.

Another confusing term is "single action." Single action means that the hammer must be cocked back before a pistol can be fired. Old-style revolvers and most older automatics could only be fired in a single-action mode; the plus for the automatics was that the reloading action also cocked the hammer automatically.

Most modern revolvers and many newer automatics fire double action. The hammer can be

1

moved back to its cocked position by pulling the trigger part way (the first action) and can then be dropped to fire the weapon as the trigger pull is completed (the second action), although there is normally no break between the two operations; it feels like one continuous pull. Most double-action pistols can also be fired in a single-action mode and nearly all double-action automatics fire in the single-action mode after the initial shot. Single-action shots are generally more accurate because less pressure and movement are needed to drop the hammer; on the flip side, single-action shots are more easily fired accidentally when one is "hyped up" with adrenaline in close-range combat. There are trade-offs with both single and double action.

If you need to bring an automatic pistol into action quickly, the old-style single-action mechanism can be a handicap, if not downright dangerous. To be really safe, many of these pistols must be carried with the chamber empty; but cycling the action to load the weapon is noisy and time-consuming. If the weapon is carried with a round in the chamber, it is dangerous to carry it with the hammer down. Even with a spring-loaded inertial firing pin that only strikes the cartridge primer after receiving a heavy blow, dropping the weapon on the hammer could still cause it to fire as could dropping it from a great height onto the barrel. Unless the pistol has an internal firing-pin block, it should not be carried with a round in the chamber and the hammer down. This brings us to the way single-action automatics are generally carried—with the hammer back and the safety locked on. The pistol can be quickly drawn and the safety flicked off when ready to fire. This mode of carry, called "cocked and locked," looks rather dangerous, but provided the safety isn't accidentally released, it is actually relatively safe.

In addition to the problem with accidental release of the safety or the outside possibility of the pistol firing if dropped on either hammer or muzzle, it is possible that the sear might break and release the hammer or, in the latter case, the firing pin might obtain enough momentum to fire the cartridge. Dirt can also get trapped between the hammer and firing pin to make firing impossible. While all these problems may be rare, in an age of lawsuits and product liability, "cocked and locked" can give users, commanding officers, insurance companies, and firearms manufacturers pause.

To get around these dangers and to simplify

bringing the weapon into play, the double-action automatic was created. The best of these employ an internal safety that blocks the firing pin; the pistol can't fire even if dropped with the safety off. Less ideal double-action pistols only block the hammer from the firing pin and have nearly all the inherent dangers of the old single-action automatic. Unfortunately, most of these pistols also have a slide-mounted safety and hammer drop which make them dangerous to carry either with the hammer down and safety off or cocked and locked. These pistols actually complicate things by making the safety hard to release and the trigger harder to pull on double action.

Fortunately, manufacturers have started using internal safeties that allow double-action automatics to be safely carried and fired without fumbling with regular safety. This type of automatic pistol fires with the ease of a revolver and is as safe as a destructive tool can be.

Modern automatics are fed from a box magazine. (Sometimes these are mistakenly called "clips." In fact, a clip is a strip of metal that holds cartridges, usually by their rims, so that they can be stripped into a magazine. While such clips are rare with pistols today, they are used with rifles and were also common with old style automatic pistols that had their magazines built into the pistol. With modern detachable magazines, it's as easy to carry a spare magazine as it is to carry a clip. Thus, clips are rarely seen with pistols.)

The placement of the magazine release varies from company to company. For larger pistols, the best place seems to be to the rear of the trigger guard on the edge of the grip panel; probably the unhandiest is at the base of the pistol grip. Unfortunately, many otherwise fine larger-caliber pistols are marred by placing the release at the bottom of the grip.

On small pocket autos or hide-away guns, the magazine release is often best located at the base of the grip, because such pistols are often carried concealed without the protection of a holster, and a chance bump could release the magazine. Too, these are last-ditch, close-range weapons, so the need to reload in combat is unlikely. Therefore, the base-of-the-grip release is ideal for many smaller automatics chambered for .22 LR, .25 ACP, and even some smaller .32 and .380 ACP pistols.

The current trend seems to be toward the larger 15-, 18-, or even 20-round magazine capacities, which give the user great firepower, but also often create pistols with rather fat grips and a lot of extra loaded weight. Pistols with large-capacity magazines are often inadequate for concealed uses, or for persons with small hands.

Machine pistols are only touched upon in this book. The term machine pistol is not a little bit confusing, partly because, in many European countries, it refers to a submachine gun. East Germany even uses the term *maschinen pistole* to describe the AK assault rifle. In this book, a machine pistol is a pistol available in a selective-fire version, such as the H&K VP-70 and Beretta 93-R.

This brings us to the assault pistol, a submachine gun whose stock and barrel are bobbed off to leave a pistol-like weapon. Modern variants make extensive use of plastics to bring their weight into the three- to four-pound range. Generally, assault pistols are blowback operated, with large upper receivers and bolts that move inside the receiver rather than the usual pistol's external slide. Assault pistol magazine capacities are in the 20- to 40-round range. The weapons are charged with a cocking handle rather than a slide. While assault pistols may see some use among tank crews and the like, their bulk and weight make them unlikely to replace the standard automatic as a sidearm for most normal use.

Assault rifles and submachine guns may seem to be replacing pistols on the modern battlefield. However, the pistol always tends to disappear from military arsenals during periods of peace; when war breaks out, troops often discover that they need pistols for some tasks in which larger weapons are impractical to carry.Whenever a compact weapon is needed, a pistol of some type is usually called for. So while pistols may not be found in the military in as great numbers as they once were, it is doubtful that they will ever vanish altogether.

And things don't remain static. Firearms development is an ongoing process, and pistols are no exception. While military handguns have not become heavier in recent years, larger magazines have given them greater firepower; and while labor costs have made extensive machining of metal parts impossible, computer-controlled machinery and the use of plastics and alloys have kept manufacturing costs down without sacrificing reliability.

Likewise, innovations in bullet design and advances in powder composition make modern ammunition capable of much greater lethality than that of a few decades ago, making handguns capable of handling bigger jobs.

Even if, for some reason, handguns should dwindle on the battlefield, they certainly aren't in danger of doing so on the home front. The Justice Department's Bureau of Justice Statistics reported recently that one out of every 31 persons over 12 years old is victimized by violent crime each year; many citizens are becoming aware of the need for self-defense. For many, a handgun concealed in the pocket, purse, or holster is an ideal way to combat crime. Likewise the handgun tends to be the weapon of choice of homeowners. Consequently, the number of pistols sold in the United States is at an all-time high.

While the revolver has vanished from the battlefield because of its sensitivity to dirt, it is still in wide use among citizens and police departments who don't want to fool with magazines, safeties, etc. The revolver can be loaded and placed in a safe place, ready to use at a moment's notice. New double-action automatics with internal safeties, however, offer much of the ease of use the revolver enjoys as well as greater firepower and reduced recoil. While the revolver will never be completely replaced, automatics could make great inroads into its market.

The bottom line for combat automatic pistols is how well they work for their intended purpose. Unfortunately, many guns sold for combat are often poor even as plinkers, and while better than nothing, are far from ideal. Anyone who may need a combat pistol needs to take a long hard look at what is available.

Like many people in the United States, I've felt the need for a good defense pistol, and in my search for an ideal weapon, I've received all sorts of advice, good and bad, and tried out all types of weapons—also good and bad. Many pistols are excellent, most have at least a few shortcomings, and some are outright disasters in both design and execution. At best, most weapons are a compromise, and automatic pistols are no exception, but different people have different needs and different manufacturers make different compromises. Getting the right pistol can shift the odds in the user's favor in combat; purchasing the wrong one can spell the user's doom.

A point to keep in mind when purchasing several pistols is whether there will be a carryover of the shooting skills you develop with each one. The old saw, "Beware the one-gun man," was true for a reason: when switching from one weapon to another, the change in point of aim, type of safety, and other factors can create problems. If you must have several guns, they should be as similar as possible in operation.

For example, imagine that you own an automatic that has no safety, or can be safely carried with the safety off; you practice with a small .22 with a different grip angle and a frame safety; and you sometimes carry a hide-away automatic with a frame safety and a magazine release on its grip base. Habits you develop with one gun may get you killed in combat. Under stress, you may not find the safety until too late or, if you get past that hurdle, you may use the point of aim of the target .22 and miss your target.

You don't have time to fumble around when you need a pistol to defend yourself. Modern gunfights happen quickly and often at short range. A recent U.S. Justice Department study found that 72 percent of police officers killed with firearms were shot within ten feet of the criminal wielding the weapon, and the majority between 8:00 P.M. and 2:00 A.M. At those ranges, there is little time to aim and often a gun's sights can't be seen at all. Instinctive shooting is important at ranges under ten feet and can only be developed by extended practice. (Julio Santiago's excellent instinctive night-shooting/target system is listed in the appendix.)

If you're going to be using firearms in combat, you don't want to spend a lot of time in slow-paced target shooting and you don't want to do a lot of shooting with dissimilar weapons. While it is good to know how various pistols work, you should be able to fire your "carry" pistol instinctively. To do so, the different pistols you shoot should have the same basic placement of safety, magazine release, etc., and the same weight, size, and grip angle. Using a "family" of similar weapons is important to develop skills and enjoy the flexibility of different calibers—and to survive a gun battle.

Unfortunately, some poorly designed firearms in today's marketplace seem to support the idea that manufacturers never went broke underestimating the needs of the shooter. There's no easy way to sort the bad pistols out from the many excellent combat automatics. Many poor pistols look great and many good pistols look ordinary. Many pistols which get great reviews in gun magazines are poorly suited to combat. You must consider both what you need and what is available; your needs may not be the same as someone else's. Take care when choosing a firearm and give thought to what features are best for *you*.

A lot of firearms are all but perfect thanks to good design, careful manufacture, and quality materials. I've written this book to help you find the pistol that is right for your needs, and I hope you'll find the same enjoyment and interest I have as you read of the strange handguns that have been developed to help people protect themselves.

A Historical Glimpse

Handguns of one type or another date back nearly as far as rifles, perhaps further, since some knights carried a mace with a built-in black powder pistol that allowed them to shoot as well as bash their enemies. From the beginning, pistols have been of great use to those who couldn't carry a large firearm, such as generals, cavalry troops, and gunners. Citizens of the past also often needed an "equalizer" stashed in a waistband or pocket. By the 1700s, no gentleman traveled without at least a pocket pistol with a six- to eight-inch barrel, pockets being somewhat larger back then.

Because of the handgun's short barrel and the demand for firepower among travelers and other citizens who might face a number of assailants, the multi-shot pistol was developed between 1600 and 1700. This development gave the fighter the ability to fire multiple shots before having to reload, and reloading was no easy process in the black powder muzzle loaders of the day.

One variation of the multiple-shot concept was the revolver. While many people think that Samuel Colt was responsible for its development, in fact there were working revolvers around 1650 and some early American colonists carried flintlock revolvers. These early revolvers were fragile, however, and not very popular for that reason.

A step up in reliability was the "pepper box" pistol. The pepper box featured multiple barrels, often bored from a single block of metal, which could be rotated into position and fired by a single hammer or, occasionally, a pair of them. With the development of the percussion cap in the early 1800s, the pepper box became very popular, since it was easy to carry and use. By 1830, the British gun maker Joseph Lang had created a pepperbox which rotated the barrels into firing position by the action of the trigger rather than by manual indexing. Pepperbox pistols weren't without their faults, however. They were heavy, due to the multiple barrels, and the hammer had to drop from above, making it impossible to aim and thus nearly impossible to use for long-range shooting.

In 1835, when Colt patented his "revolver" in Britain and the United States, a huge market quickly developed for the pistol that was lighter and tougher than other multiple-shot handguns of the period. However, the Colt revolver was still slow to reload. After five shots (the sixth cylinder generally being left empty by those who were safety conscious), the shooter either had to remove the cylinder and drop in a previously charged one (the black powder equivalent of the speed loader) or go through the laborious process of reloading each chamber with percussion cap, powder, and ball.

Reloading time was reduced when metallic cartridges were developed. The primer, powder, and ball were placed in a container (usually copper or brass, though paper and other materials were tried with varying degrees of success) which could load a cylinder in one step. As more emphasis was placed on the quick reloading of revolvers, new methods of loading and unloading were developed; break-top and swing-out cylinder arrangements greatly speeded things up.

But the capacity of any revolver is physically limited to five to seven rounds in most larger calibers if the weapon is to remain a practical size. While some work was done with double rows of cartridges, this arrangement only succeeded in creating monstrosities that were far from handy to shoot. So, in effect, the revolver soon reached the height of its capability. New revolvers showed improvements in durability, firing speed (with double-action triggers), and convenience but still suffered from the firepower limitation.

As the single-action black powder revolver reached its zenith during the late 1800s, new automated weapons like the Gatling gun started to appear, but were seriously hampered by poor materials and ammunition. Dependable portable weapons like the semiauto pistol, machine gun, and combat rifle all had to wait for smokeless powder, stronger alloys, and more precise machining techniques. Thus, the creation of the modern semiauto pistol coincides with the height of the industrial revolution and the development of modern chemical industries.

With the creation of modern steels and chemicals at the end of the 1800s, there was a virtual explosion in automatic pistol design, with weapons like the Mauser, Borchardt, Bergmann, and Browning quickly establishing records for firepower and reliability from 1895 through the early 1900s. The same period produced a number of dead ends, including the automatic revolver. This weapon used a recoiling barrel and cylinder to cock its hammer and index the cylinder. This absurd weapon has fortunately vanished from everything but fictional stories.

Likewise, design suffered from the ideas of the past. Just as revolver and rifle magazines were placed ahead of the trigger/grip area, so too, most early automatic pistol designs placed the magazine in front of the trigger. This allowed the shape and angle of the grip to be whatever was practical and comfortable and also helped control recoil. Unfortunately, human engineering was not a consideration during this period, and nearly all these weapons are saddled with awkward "broomhandle" grips, misplaced safeties, and long barrels. These design flaws doomed these weapons over the long run.

As smokeless powder reduced the size of the pistol cartridge, designers found that the magazine well could be placed in the grip. The magazine well is easily found for reloading with a hand-finds-hand movement, the weapon is more compact, and the barrel can be longer while the overall length is still reduced. Designers like Browning were soon placing the slide release, magazine release, and safety in positions that allowed quick and easy one-handed operation.

John Moses Browning was perhaps the most influential of all the turn-of-the-century gun designers. In addition to his pistols, this prolific American inventor created the Winchester Models 1886/71/1894 lever action rifles, the 1895 "Potato Digger" machine gun, the Browning Automatic Rifle (1917), the Auto Five shotgun (1902), and the Browning .30- and .50-caliber machine guns (1918)—most of which remain in use to this day!

Among Browning's more important pistol designs are the Model 1900, 1905, and 1911 Colts, the FN 1903 pistol, the FN M1910 pistol (in .32/.380 Auto), the .25 ACP Colt/FN pocket pistol, the Colt "Woodsman," and the FN Hi-Power. Possibly the last of his designs is yet to be seen: a number of pistols to which Colt and Fabrique Nationale purchased the patent rights were never manufactured. There is no reason to think the designs were inferior. Rather, the patents were purchased and held onto to prevent other companies from competing with Colt and FN. Seven of Colt's patent rights for Browning pistols were never exercised and have since expired.

Browning wasn't the only influential designer. In Germany, Carl Walther and his sons Erich, Fritz, and George had started designing and selling pistols in 1907. In 1929, they first offered the "Polizei Pistole" or "PP." This automatic could be safely carried with the safety off, thanks to an internal firing-pin block, and had a quick-to-use double-action trigger. The Walther pistol had all the advantages of a revolver and few of the disadvantages.

In addition to variations of the PP's basic design (it seems that about every third .380 ACP pistol available is a PP variation), its double-action trigger and slide-mounted, dropping-hammer safety are still found on the majority of modern double-action automatics.

Modern automatics are now being made with large-capacity magazines which pack a lot of firepower into a small weapon. The assault rifle/submachine gun magazine on the left holds 36 rounds, while modern automatic magazines like that on the right hold from 13 to 18 rounds without using an extended magazine.

One might easily argue that few innovations have taken place since the 1930s. Staggered, large-capacity magazines, double-action triggers, and hammer drop/firing-pin block safeties had all been developed by the 1930s. In fact, many early pistols, like the Browning Hi-Power and Walther P-38, continue in use today and are often considered "state of the art" with just a little tinkering in finish and materials. "New" automatics are generally rearrangements of various features of these and other pistols coupled with new alloys or even plastics and modern manufacturing techniques. Browning or the Walthers would need to learn little to start designing new guns today.

Modern automatics operate with either a blowback action or some type of locking mechanism. Generally, blowback operation is used in pistols chambered for small cartridges. Blowback operation uses the slide's inertia and a recoil spring to keep the chamber closed until the bullet has left the barrel and pressures have dropped to a safe level.

With larger cartridges, recoil is greater, so that a locking system is used to keep the chamber closed until the pressure drops. The most common of these are the short recoil system, retarded blowback, and—occasionally—gas operation. These methods are found on most combat automatics except for small hide-away guns and the like.

The majority of automatics use a hammer which strikes a firing pin; even many "hammerless" automatics actually have an internal hammer inside the frame. Other automatics use a "striker," a spring-loaded firing pin released by the trigger pull. (The striker flies forward to directly strike the primer of the cartridge.) The striker system is most common in small-caliber pistols, but this is certainly not a hard-and-fast rule, and the use of a striker can often greatly simplify a pistol's design.

Many of Browning's early pistols were devoid of safety systems other than the inertial firing pin, which occasionally failed to prevent accidental shootings. Thus, as the end of the twentieth century approaches, safety systems have become better and simpler to operate, with many safeties operating automatically.

As dirt, rubble, and mud became hallmarks of twentieth-century warfare, firearms had to endure mud and dampness unknown in previous wars. During this period the automatic pistol—whose mechanism was fairly well sealed from dirt—proved to be ideally suited for combat. Unlike the revolver, which tended to become full of grime and dirt, and whose cartridges were exposed to the elements, most automatic pistols excluded dirt from their actions and kept their cartridges safe and sound in a sealed magazine. Another plus for the automatic was that it could be easily taken apart and cleaned or even repaired in the field. Such was not the case with the revolver until very recently. The contrasts between the revolver and automatic made lasting impressions on troops and decision-makers alike. By World War II, the automatic had all but replaced the revolver on the battlefield.

In the post-war period, it was gradually realized that the automatic pistol was also capable of great accuracy and, again bettering the revolver, fired bullets with greater and more consistent velocity. As automatics picked up a double-action mode and simpler safety systems during the 1970s and 1980s, automatic pistols appeared in the hands of urban policemen and special officers, especially since the automatic's thin body made it more easily concealable than the revolver.

Another trend over the last two centuries is toward smaller calibers. The driving forces behind this trend were smokeless powders and better bullet design. Where bores of .45 or even .80 were needed to do much damage to an opponent when using black powder, with modern smokeless powders bore sizes gradually became smaller and smaller. Many smaller caliber weapons are capable of as much damage as many of the older large-bore black powder guns. In addition to the caliber decrease, cartridges have also become smaller overall since smokeless powder can develop more power in a smaller space. While automatic pistol chamberings have remained pretty much the same during this century, modifications in bullet nose configuration have made modern bullets much more deadly than their round-nose, full-metal-jacket (FMJ) ancestors.

The detachable stock was popular in the U.S. on revolvers during the mid-1800s (some stocks featured built-in canteens or coffee grinders), and resurfaced in the early 1900s on early Lugers, Brownings, Mausers, and Berettas. In theory, a pistol stock creates a rifle-like weapon from a handgun, but the idea seems to work only on paper. Armies adopt the system and drop it with stunning regularity, but the detachable stock seems like a good idea and is found on many of the newest pistols. New lightweight plastic or folding stocks, three-round burst modes, and the addition of a forward grip (perhaps over the muzzle so that the pistol is held sideways when being fired with sights mounted on the side of the pistol) all change the pistol's capability. Whether these innovations will make the stocked "machine pistol" an ideal weapon and whether there is a large enough market for such pistols remains to be seen. Nevertheless, many large manufacturers are hedging their bets with stocked pistols just in case a demand for them develops.

Laws can also change firearms trends. If, under certain laws, a market can be reached with one type of firearm but not another, manufacturers have no choice but to conform to those laws. Thus, the embargo by the major powers on shipments of rifles to China in the early 1900s created a ready market for stocked pistols, a market supplied by Mauser, FN, Astra, and others.

At the other extreme, stocked pistols created such fear among uninformed legislators of the 1930s that they outlawed the unauthorized use of a stock on any weapon in the United States with a barrel length of less than 16 inches. Likewise, the Gun Control Act (GCA) of 1968 banned the importation of many small pistols, but allowed the manufacture or assembly of such pistols in the United States. This has led to limitations in the size of pistols made outside the United States if the manufacturer intends to capture a share of the lucrative American market.

Fear of lawsuits also leads to changes in firearms. The recent rash of legal actions has created a few "super safe" pistols which make it almost impossible to get off a first shot in combat. However, as manufacturers split the difference between legal considerations and combat necessity, almost any modern pistol now sports some or all of the following: half-cock notch which prevents accidentally dropping the hammer on a loaded chamber; loaded chamber indicator; spring-loaded firing pin; disconnector to prevent firing a round when the slide isn't locked; firing-pin block (or two); and maybe even some dubious feature like a grip or magazine safety, which prevents firing the weapon with the magazine removed. While some automatic pistol designs do a poor job of incorporating these, others create an extremely safe but easy-to-use weapon.

As technology changes, there will undoubtedly be further changes in automatic pistols. While it's hard to imagine many major design innovations, a

Assault pistols like the TEC-9 (left) are similar to modern automatics like the P7-M13. While assault pistols may see some use among tank crews, it is doubtful that the assault pistol will displace the standard automatic as a side arm for most of the situations in which a pistol is normally used due to its size and weight.

number of minor changes are certainly waiting in the wings. Plastics and caseless ammunition promise potentially new, simplified, and lightweight weapons. Kevlar fiber (the stronger-than-steel material used in "bulletproof" vests) may be employed to create nearly all-plastic weapons with metal used only for the springs and perhaps a barrel liner inside a Kevlar/resin barrel. Also possible, though perhaps not practical, would be ceramic barrels wrapped with Kevlar bands to contain the pressure of the detonating cartridge. Perhaps the all-plastic disposable pistol isn't that far away!

But pistols of the near future may not even be made of plastic. With investment casting methods and computer-controlled machinery cutting down on the costs of manufacturing metal parts, the "look" of machined metal in firearms may make a comeback and displace a lot of the market that is now threatened by relatively inexpensive plastic and sheet metal guns. The twenty-first century may even reveal an as-yet-undiscovered type of firearm, the way the twentieth century did with the automatic pistol; today's high-tech pistol may be tomorrow's museum piece.

Regardless of what the future may bring, a wide variety of combat automatic pistols is available in today's marketplace. Let's take a look at some of these pistols.

.22 Long Rifle and .25 ACP

John Browning developed the .25 ACP to provide reliable functioning in automatic pistols which just couldn't function on the black-powder .22 cartridges of his day. Since then, the .22 LR has come a long way; pistols designed for it are usually every bit as reliable as their .25 ACP counterparts, and the .22 has become a more potent round with the introduction of new powders and bullet design. In fact, some newer .22 loads like CCI's "Stinger" are actually more potent than the .25 ACP. Coupled with the much lower cost of .22 ammunition, there is little reason to go with the .25 ACP unless you're willing to shell out some extra money for one of the new, potent "hot" loads.

Of course there's a catch to the pluses of the .22. There is a wide variance in ammunition, with some cartridges loaded to the old black-powder tolerances and other high-velocity .22s loaded to hotter specs. This means that many .22 automatics are a bit finicky about what type of ammunition they take. Therefore, it's a good idea to try out a pistol with a variety of ammunition immediately after purchasing it. If a .22 pistol won't function reliably with high-performance ammo, then it isn't of much use in combat.

Perhaps the most popular combat .22/.25 pistols are the hide-away or "pocket" guns, which can be concealed in ways impossible with larger weapons. Being pocket pistols, these guns are normally fired at close range without aiming and a high sight could get snagged on the user's clothing. Poor sights, or even none at all, are a plus with guns made to be concealed. Likewise, a magazine release at the base of the pistol grip is ideal with hide-away pistols since it prevents accidental release of the magazine.

A number of .22 and .25 pistols are larger than the pocket pistol and similar firearms chambered in .32 or .380 ACP. It makes little sense to purchase a .22 or .25 pistol which is no smaller than the more powerful models. Therefore, all things being equal, it's best to use larger caliber weapons when they're available.

The exception to this rule is the "trainer" automatic pistol, which may be very similar to a large-caliber combat handgun. Such weapons offer a means of developing marksmanship or instinctive shooting skills without the expense of center-fire ammunition, and can often be created by modifying the grip of standard pistols like the Ruger Mark

11

II, or, if you're arming yourself with the .32 or .380, then the .22/.25 "look alike" would make sense for practice.

Finally, a third type of pistol is the .22 automatic capable of good accuracy and often coupled with a silencer for clandestine use. Such pistols are generally larger than hide-away guns and function more reliably. These pistols will usually have excellent sights and accuracy when compared to the pocket pistols or practice handguns.

While a pistol chambered for either the .22 LR or the .25 ACP doesn't have much to offer in the way of "stopping power" compared to a large-caliber handgun, it is certainly better than no firearm at all. These calibers wound by puncturing. If you can imagine being stabbed by a foot-long ice pick, you have some idea of the wound these bullets can create. Bullet placement is essential when using .22/.25 rounds for defense. Therefore, anyone using one of these pistols for self-defense had better be capable of using it to good effect in a combat encounter.

In the pocket pistol group, the Jennings J-22 (.22 LR) and Raven (.25 ACP) are probably the best buys; the choice of practice pistols will depend on the type of large-caliber firearm you are using, though the Ruger Mark II, Browning Challenger, or Iver Johnson Trailsman are excellent choices if properly modified.

In the target pistol/clandestine use category, it is my opinion that the Ruger Mark II is the runaway first choice.

The Raven .25 auto (top right) and its sister gun, the Jennings J-22 in .22 LR, are probably the best buys in pocket pistols. The principal difference between the two is that the Raven is more squared off and has the extractor located at the top of its slide rather than at the side.

For inexpensive practice with .22 LR ammunition, the Ruger Mark II pistol is a good buy. And in the target pistol/clandestine use category, the Ruger Mark II is the runaway first choice.

AMT BACKUP

This pistol is also available in .380 ACP. The manual safety is placed where one would expect to find a magazine-release button, while the magazine release is located at the grip base. A heavy trigger pull and a grip safety allow one to carry the pistol with the manual safety in the fire position.

Unfortunately, field-stripping is complicated and requires the use of an Allen wrench and other tools. The heavy trigger pull makes this pistol slightly less accurate than one might hope. For extra concealability, the magazine finger rest might be removed. This is probably not the first choice for a hide-away gun.

Specifications

Overall length: 4.25 in.
Weight (unloaded): 1.13 lbs.
Barrel length: 2.5 in.
Magazine capacity: 5 (8 rounds in .22 LR)

AMT LIGHTNING

This pistol is a copy of the Sturm, Ruger Mark II. The principle differences are a more squared-off receiver and a spike on the front of the trigger guard which looks like part of a brass knuckle. The pistol also has mounting cuts for scope rings on the receiver, an adjustable trigger, and rubber Pachmayr grips. Like the Ruger Mark II, the pistol has a slide release at the top of the left pistol grip. Also like the Ruger, the Lightning points well and is a good choice as a target or practice/teaching pistol, or possibly for clandestine use.

The AMT Lightning is available in a wide range of barrel lengths (5, 6-1/2, 8-1/2, 10, and 12-1/2 inches) and styles. The heavy bull barrel is used by many target shooters because it soaks up recoil and builds up the wrist muscles. The trade-off is that the pistol is heavy; it weighs as much as many large-caliber weapons. Adjustable target sights are available at additional cost on all models.

The longer-barrel models are of somewhat

dubious use since the .22 round gains maximum velocity with an eight- to ten-inch barrel. However, the longer barrel can reduce muzzle retort for quiet shooting with CCI CB caps.

The AMT Lightning is a good pistol, but it seems to be slightly inferior to the original Ruger in both functioning and finish. It is probably best to purchase the Lightning only if it offers something the Ruger pistols don't; why purchase a copy when you can have the original for a little more?

The specifications and takedown of the AMT are nearly identical to the Ruger Mark II. Many Ruger accessories will also fit the Lightning.

ASTRA CONSTABLE

This pistol is available in .380 ACP as well as .22 LR, and is loosely designed around the Walther PP. Constable pistols have a rather poor reputation for reliability.

Specifications

Overall length: 6.69 in.
Weight (unloaded): 1.5 lbs.
Barrel length: 3.5 in.
Magazine capacity: 10

The Beretta 418 has a grip safety which duplicates the curve of the back of the grip. The 418s have a striker indicator hole in the rear of the slide that allows you to see that the striker is cocked and ready to fire. This 418 was imported into the United States and sold as the "Panther" model. The 418s are ideal if you need a reliable .25 ACP pistol.

BABY BROWNING

The Baby Browning appeared in the early 1920s. It was based on Browning's 1906 model but lacked its grip safety and rounded shape. The magazine release is located at the grip base, and the safety is a lever just ahead of the left grip plate.

This pistol is no longer available now in the United States because of the 1968 GCA, though it may still be found used. New similar pistols are being made by Fraser Firearms ("Fraser Automatic Pistol") and by Precision Small Parts ("PSP-25/22"). The PSP-25/22 is an interesting variation that can be converted from .22 Short to .25 ACP by changing the barrel, magazine, and firing pin, but unless you need the capability, it is probably better not to fool with the .22 Short conversion.

The Baby Browning and its variants have little to offer that can't be found on other, less expensive pistols like the Raven and Jennings J-22, and are probably better left to the collector.

BERETTA (1919), 318/418

These little pistols date back to 1919, when Beretta first tried to capture part of the pocket pistol market. The most desirable of these are the later models with the grip safety, which allows the pistol to be carried with the manual safety off (this is not as safe as having the manual safety on, but it also allows a quick first shot which may be of prime concern if the pistol is needed in a hurry).

The Model 318 has a humped grip safety, while the 418's safety duplicates the curve of the back of the grip. Late 318s and all 418s have a striker cocking indicator hole in the rear of the slide (this is *not* a loaded chamber indicator). The 418s were marketed in the United States under the "Bantam" trademark which was later changed to "Panther." Some 418s were made with alloy frames which cut the weapon's overall weight by three ounces.

Late model 318s and all 418s are good reliable .25 ACP pistols. Disassembly is similar to that of the 1935 listed in the .32/.380 section.

Specifications

    Overall length: 4.56 inches
    Weight (unloaded): 0.93 lbs.
                       (0.73 lbs. alloy receiver)
    Barrel length: 2.36 inches
    Magazine capacity: 8

BERETTA 948

The 948 is nearly identical to the .32/.380 Model 1935. Unfortunately it lacks the 1935's half-cock notch in the hammer. This, coupled with the lack of an inertial firing pin, makes the 948 impossible to carry with the safety off and a round in the chamber. Several long-barreled target versions of this .22 model were also offered. One was a kit gun with a standard and a 6-inch barrel; the other was the 949 target pistol. None of these are suitable for concealment, but the 949 might be considered for silenced use or for practice if you own the similar 1935.

BERETTA 950

The Beretta 950 is available in .25 ACP and .22 Short; in the United States, the .22 version was often imported and marketed as the Minx and the .25 as the Jetfire. Don't bother with the Minx/.22 Short version; it doesn't have the punch needed in combat.

Both pistols have a tip-up barrel which allows them to be loaded without cycling the slide or used as a single-shot target gun. However, this feature can also create problems. If a round misfires, it is necessary to flip the barrel open and remove the shell. If the shell isn't ejected by opening the barrel, it has to be pried out by hand, since the pistol has no extractor. Then the barrel has to be locked back down and the slide cycled to load a new round and cock the hammer. This is too slow and complex an operation for a close combat weapon. Perhaps the 950's worst shortcoming, however, is that it lacks any safety other than a half-cock notch on the hammer. With an inertial firing pin, this makes carrying the pistol a rather risky proposition.

The magazine release is located at the lower left of the grip. The barrel release is on the left of the receiver just behind the trigger guard.

The 950 series of pistols is probably best passed up; if you like the quality of the Beretta pistols, try the Models 20/21 listed below—they are nearly identical to the 950 but have a manual safety.

BERETTA 20/21 (A)

The Model 20 (.25 ACP) and the Model 21 (.22 LR) were both developed from the 950 series. Like the 950, the 20 and 21 both have barrels that

The 950 series of Beretta pistols is available in .25 ACP and .22 Short; both models of the pistol have a tip-up barrel which allows the pistol to be loaded without cycling the slide or using the pistol as a single-shot target gun. This feature can also create problems in combat should a round misfire. If the shell isn't flipped out with the opening of the barrel, it has to be pried out by hand, since the pistol has no extractor.

The Beretta 950 pistol chambered in .22 Short was often imported and marketed as the "Minx." The Minx/.22 Short just doesn't have the punch needed in combat except, perhaps, for covert use.

The Beretta 950 pistol chambered in .22 Short just doesn't have the punch needed in combat except, perhaps, for clandestine use coupled with a silencer. Shown here is a Minx in combination with a Jonathon Arthur Ciener silencer. Photo courtesy of Jonathon Arthur Ciener.

tip up for reloading. The barrel still lacks an extractor, making it mandatory to keep the weapon very clean, and uses reliable ammunition. The barrel release lever is located on the left of the pistol just behind the trigger guard. When the release is tripped, the barrel springs up; the force of its opening will usually eject the shell in the barrel.

Unlike the 950, these models have a double-action trigger and a manual thumb safety located on the left rear of the frame. These allow for a safe carry while also guaranteeing that they can be brought into action quickly. The double-action trigger also allows a cartridge to be "tapped" a second time if it fails to fire.

The magazine release is located in the lower rear area of the left grip panel. The 20 has black plastic grips and a sharp rear curve at the base of the grip and lacks a half-cock notch in its hammer. The 21 has wooden grips with a more rounded back strap and has a half-cock notch.

For a time the 20/21 pistols weren't available to U.S. shooters without special permits, thanks to the 1968 GCA, but they are now being made in the U.S. Beretta plant. Recently the 21 models have been designated the "21A." Both are identical; the suffix was apparently added because a "B" model may be added later on. (Currently Beretta appears to be planning to discontinue the Model 20 and manufacture the Model 21 in .22 LR and .25 ACP. Possibly the "21B" will be the pistol in its .25 ACP chambering.)

The Beretta 21/21A is ammunition-sensitive. This, coupled with the need to tilt the barrel up to remove a round, means that you must be sure to test out ammunition and find the type that works best. With the 21/21A, the Winchester Wildcat and Remington High Velocity will probably function well. Both the 20 and 21/21A are ideal hide-away pistols if kept clean and fed reliable ammunition.

Field-stripping is simple: remove the magazine and cycle the weapon to be sure it's empty and leave the hammer cocked; release the barrel so that it pops up and swing it forward as far as it will easily go; pull the slide back slightly and lift its front end up so that it can clear the barrel brackets; push the slide forward off its frame rails and remove it. Reassembly is basically a reversal of this procedure.

Specifications for Model 20

Overall length: 4.5 inches
Weight (unloaded): 0.69 lbs.
Barrel length: 2.4 inches
Magazine capacity: 8

Specifications for Model 21/21A

Overall length: 4.9 inches
Weight (unloaded): 0.77 lbs.
Barrel length: 2.5 inches
Magazine capacity: 7

BERETTA SERIES 71 PISTOL

This is one of the series 70 pistols described in the .32/.380 chapter. It was introduced in 1958. Because it is as large as its sister .32 and .380 pistols, the others would be better combat choices, though the 71 might be useful for practice.

BERETTA MODEL 87BB

The 87BB is the .22 LR version of the 80-series pistols chambered in .32/.380. While not a good combat pistol, the 87BB is an ideal training aid, since it is so similar to both the Beretta 92 series of 9mm Luger pistols as well as the other 80-series pistols.

BERNARDELLI USA

The USA is based on the Walther PPK and is available in .32 and .380 as well as .22 LR. The more powerful chamberings would probably be a better choice than the .22 LR model.

BROWNING CHALLENGER

In 1962, Browning Firearms introduced three .22 pistols which outwardly resembled the Colt Challenger version of the Woodsman. The new pistols were slightly modified internally under the direction of Bruce Browning, the grandson of John Browning. One of these three new pistols was the Challenger, a target pistol with adjustable trigger and rear sight. The Nomad was the economy model, with a 4-1/2 or later 6-1/2 inch barrel. The Medalist was designed for competition shooters with a contoured walnut grip, vented 6-3/4 inch barrel, and weights to vary its balance as well as an adjustable sight and dry-firing mechanism.

In 1970, the International Medalist was introduced. This was a Medalist pistol with thinned fore-end and thinner grip. All versions of the pistol were discontinued in 1974 because they couldn't be manufactured at competitive prices.

The Challenger II was marketed in 1976. It is a slightly modified version of the original pistol, overhauled by Joe Badali. To keep costs down, this pistol was manufactured in the United States rather than in Belgium. It has a matte finish, an adjustable rear sight, round barrel, laminated grip panels, a bolt hold-open lever, and a 6-3/4 inch round barrel similar to that of the original Woodsman.

In 1982, the Challenger III was introduced with a squared-off 5-1/2 inch bull barrel, a lightweight alloy frame, and new sights. By the mid-1980s, the Challenger III had been modified to become the Challenger III Sporter, and a low-cost version with plastic grip panels and a simplified rear sight, the

In 1982, Browning introduced the Challenger III .22 LR pistol. It has a 5½-inch bull barrel and a lightweight alloy frame. Like other Browning firearms, the Challenger III pistols are well made and worthy of consideration by those who need a large, accurate .22 pistol. Photo courtesy of Browning.

Browning introduced a low-cost version of its .22 pistols in 1985. With plastic grip panels and a simplified rear sight, the "Buck Mark .22" is a good buy and may be of special appeal to many shooters due to its price and the button magazine release on the left grip panel behind the trigger guard. Photo courtesy of Browning.

Buck Mark 22, was introduced in 1985. (Many shooters will prefer the Buck Mark 22 to some of the other models because of its less expensive price and the button magazine release found on the left grip panel behind the trigger guard.)

Browning pistols are well made and worthy of consideration. Given its past track record, the Challenger III may well be dropped from production or modified to other configurations before it hits its stride.

Takedown is similar to the Woodsman.

Specifications for Challenger III Sporter

Overall length: 10.88 inches
Weight (unloaded): 1.82 lbs.
Barrel length: 6.75 inches
Magazine capacity: 10

CHARTER ARMS MODEL 40

The Model 40 and its sister gun, the Model 79K, are made in Germany and imported by Charter Arms. Although based on the Walther PP, the pistol's outer layout is similar to the S&W pistols, which makes it worth considering for practice or training. It should be noted, however, that the magazine release is at the grip base rather than on the side.

For more information on this firearm, see the chapter on .32/.380 pistols.

Specifications for Model 40

Overall length: 6.3 inches
Weight (unloaded): 1.34 lbs.
Barrel length: 3.3 inches
Magazine capacity: 7

COLT WOODSMAN

The original Woodsman created by John Browning in 1911 was designed for the .22 Short. The basic pistol was designed by two Colt engineers, F. C. Chadwick and G. H. Tansley, and the gun was introduced to the public in 1915. It wasn't until 1927 that Colt started calling the pistol the "Woodsman;" before that time, it was simply known as the "Colt .22 Automatic Pistol." Despite the fact that the name wasn't used on the first models, they are all now referred to as Woodsman.

The original version was manufactured until 1943, when it was discontinued. There are two types of prewar Woodsman, the standard and the March Target Model which was marketed in 1938, with 4-1/2 or 6-1/2 inch barrels on either model. These early pistols were designed for semi-smokeless, lubricated cartridges and are not ideal for use with modern high-velocity ammunition. (An experimental, detachable stocked version was also created but never marketed.)

Production resumed in 1947 and ceased in 1977. The postwar pistols include Target and Sport models similar to the prewar weapons; the Challenger, introduced in 1950, which was a budget version of the Woodsman; the Huntsman, which replaced the Challenger in 1955; and the Targetsman, also introduced in 1955, which was a Huntsman fitted with slightly better sights, a more complex grip, and a 6 inch barrel. In general, these pistols all have a grip that is flat at the base rather than rounded and slanting as in prewar models, and the barrel lengths are 4-1/2 and 6 inches. Standard models had rounded barrels, while target models had squared, slab-sided barrels to reduce recoil.

The pistol uses simple blowback operation and

has a concealed hammer. The thumb safety also acts as a slide lock and, since it can't be engaged unless the hammer is cocked, as a cocking indicator. The magazine release is located on the rear grip base on many models, although many postwar pistols made from 1947 until 1955 have the more desirable button magazine release on the left grip.

The Woodsman pistols are well designed and well made, but have little to offer that isn't found on Iver Johnson's Trailsman, the Browning Challenger series, or the tough Ruger Mark I/IIs. Being out of production, the Colt guns are hard to find (as are parts and magazines), and to repair.

Specifications

Overall length: 10 inches
(with 6-inch barrel)
Weight (unloaded,
6-inch barrel): 2 lbs.
Barrel length: 6 inches
Magazine capacity: 10

ERMA KGP22

This is a .22 version of the Luger, similar to Erma's KGP38 in .380 ACP. The KGP22 is nice for plinking but has little to offer unless you need a practice pistol that handles like a Luger—a doubtful proposition, given the Luger's poor combat performance. This pistol is probably best avoided unless you want a "Luger" that doesn't cost as much as its 9mm counterpart.

EXCAM MODEL GT27

This .25 automatic is made in Italy and has a Beretta look to it. Finish and fit are a little crude but allow a very low retail cost. Trigger action is unbelievably heavy on some pistols, though they are generally pretty reliable.

The manual safety has to be rotated a full 180 degrees to go from safe to fire; awkward but not impossibly so, since the pistol is so small. The pistol does have an external hammer with a half-cock notch which makes it possible to carry the weapon with a round in the chamber, hammer on half-cock, and the safety off for a quick shot.

The GT27 is available in both blued and chrome finishes. While a bit crude, it is fairly reliable and makes a fair hide-away pistol. It is sometimes marketed as the Targa GT27.

Disassembly is almost too easy; occasionally the slide threatens to dismount itself when cycling a round into the chamber manually. Therefore, care has to be taken when loading. Takedown is simple: remove the magazine and cycle the action to be sure it's empty and leave the hammer cocked; rotate the thumb safety forward; pull the slide back and upward so that it is released; push the slide off the front of the frame; and remove the recoil spring and safety. Reassembly is a reversal of the above.

Specifications

Overall length: 4.5 inches
Weight (unloaded): 0.82 lbs.
Barrel length: 2.5 inches
Magazine capacity: 7

EXPLORER II

The Explorer II is a chopped version of the AR-7 (Explorer) rifle, and was first marketed by Charter Arms in 1980. The pistol looks as ugly as the old Broomhandle Mauser but is actually easy to handle thanks to its lightweight aluminum frame and barrel. (A steel insert contains the rifling.)

The AR-7 was designed as a survival rifle for the U.S. Air Force; the Explorer II has the rifle's same simple design: one-piece trigger/sear, one spring for both hammer and trigger, and a trigger/hammer assembly easily accessible by removing one screw on the side plate. The barrel is screwed onto the receiver by the user so that it is simple to change barrels. Adding to the pistol's flexibility, Charter Arms offers 6-, 8-, and 10-inch barrels. The 16-inch AR-7 rifle barrel can be adapted to the pistol by filing off the alignment lug on the barrel and replacing it with a steel screw on the opposite side. Coupled with a scope, the pistol can do the work of a .22 rifle.

One advantage is that most of the accessories available for the AR-7 rifle also fit the Explorer II pistol. This gives the owner the option of adding, among other things, a scope mount and an extended 25-round magazine (available from Ram Line). The scope mount need not be a pistol scope since the Explorer II's bolt is contained within its receiver. No slide or receiver cycles back at the shooter, so he can safely have his face right up to the pistol when looking through the scope.

All isn't rosy, however. The safety is awkward for right-handed users since it is located at the top

Since accessories designed for the AR-7 rifle fit the Charter Arms Explorer II pistol as well, there is a large number of accessories available for the Explorer II. As a result, the owner of an Explorer II has the option of adding accessories like this Tasco rifle scope and a Ram-Line 25-round magazine. (Note the d-i-y epoxy and wood finger rest added behind the trigger guard to improve the "pointing" of the pistol.) With the availability of various barrel lengths, this pistol can often be customized to the user's needs.

of the right grip. Worst of all, the grip makes it hard to instinctively point the weapon and the charging handle may drop into the receiver, making it hard to cock the weapon in a hurry, but these problems are easily solved by a do-it-yourselfer. The pistol's inexpensive price makes it a very good buy.

The first modification that is in order is filling in the space between the rear of the trigger guard and the grip. This can be done with wood and glue, epoxy putty, etc., or by making new grips which bridge the gap. Keeping the charging handle from dropping into the receiver is also simple: just cut a small link of aluminum rod to shape and drop it in under the handle when the pistol is disassembled.

Holsters for the Explorer II are nearly impossible to find. An Uncle Mike's holster made for the 10-inch barrel Ruger Mark II can be altered to fit the Explorer II, however, by cutting away part of the seam of the trigger guard area of the holster and resewing it just below the cut. If you have a 10-inch barrel, you'll also need to cut a hole in the

seam at the base of the holster and then resew the seams so they don't unravel.

Many Explorer II owners complain about feeding problems. The problem is usually that the weapon needs to have the barrel throated, which is simple thanks to the aluminum barrel. File off a small amount of metal so that the sharp edge of the chamber is rounded off. If necessary, a slight ramp can be added to the lower part of the barrel to help cartridges climb into the chamber. Be careful not to overdo a good thing; remove only a tiny amount of metal in either of these operations.

Finally, it would be wise to grind off part of the area of the safety that sticks out from the side of the pistol. This safety is prone to being accidentally switched off if the wearer bumps into something or travels through brush. Discovering you've been carrying a gun in your holster with the safety off and a round in the chamber is disconcerting at best.

The Explorer II has a lot of potential as a special-purpose .22 pistol for those who are willing to take the time to modify it slightly. It is available with either a black or a "silver" aluminum finish.

Field-stripping is simple. Remove the magazine and cycle the pistol to be sure it's empty; unscrew and remove the barrel; remove the charging handle; unscrew the side plate and remove it; remove the ejector from the trigger assembly so that the bolt can slide free; remove the bolt. This will allow you to clean all the working parts of the pistol. Reassembly is a reversal of this procedure.

Specifications

Overall length: 15.5 inches
Weight (unloaded): 1.75 lbs.
Barrel length: 8 inches
Magazine capacity: 8 (25-round available)

HECKLER & KOCH 4

This pistol is based on the old Mauser HSc which was popular before World War II in Ger-

many. The H&K was used by the German Customs Police for some time as the P11. In addition to the usual .32/.380 version, the pistol is also available in .22 LR and .25 ACP or as a kit gun which can be changed to the various calibers by exchanging the barrels, recoil springs, firing pin, and magazines. For more information, see the section on .32/.380 pistols.

HECKLER & KOCH P7-K3

This pistol is capable of firing .22 LR as well as .32 or .380 ACP, which makes it an ideal weapon for those who have a P-7 chambered in 9mm Luger. For more information, see the chapters on .32/.380 ACP and 9mm Luger pistols.

HIGH STANDARD

The High Standard Company got into guns by the back door when it acquired the tools and equipment of the bankrupt Hartford Arms Company. High Standard then produced a version of

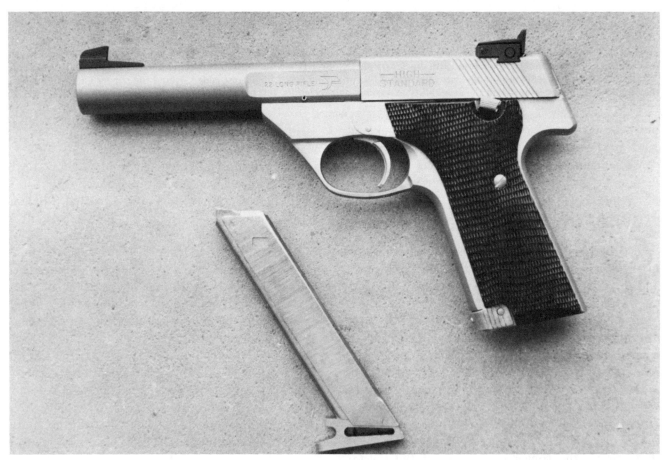

The "High Standard" was used for training recruits during World War II and employed as a covert weapon by the OSS (Office of Strategic Services) and others. The pistol also saw some use in Vietnam and enjoyed civilian sales in the United States until the mid-1980s, when the company went bankrupt.

the Hartford pistol which gradually became known for its accuracy.

The pistol was known simply as the High Standard but had a number of variations over the years. Production ceased in 1942 but was resumed the following year to make training pistols as well as a silenced version for clandestine use by the OSS and others. Following the war, the pistol was again offered to civilian buyers until the company went bankrupt in the mid-1980s.

At the time of this writing, it appears that High Standard will not go back into production. Therefore, parts will become harder to obtain and repairs more expensive. This, coupled with the fact that the Ruger Mark II pistols generally fill the same niche and in fact had a lot to do with putting High Standard out of business, probably makes the Mark II a better choice.

IVER JOHNSON TRAILSMAN TM.22PB6

When the patents expired on the Colt Woodsman pistols and production ceased in 1977, Iver Johnson sought to capture some of the market abandoned by Colt by producing a pistol nearly identical to the old Woodsman. The new pistol, called the Trailsman, was introduced in 1984.

The pistol is currently available only in a standard model with either a 4-1/2- or 6-inch barrel, the choice of blued or matte finish, and checkered or composition grip panels. The magazine release is located on the left of the frame just behind the trigger guard. On the down side is a magazine disconnector which complicates the pistol and its disassembly.

Unfortunately, a few Trailsman pistols currently on the market seem to be a little rough around the edges. If you purchase a Trailsman, give it a good workout and take it in for tuning with a gunsmith if you run into problems. The basic design is sound, but the parts fit may create problems in new pistols.

Disassembly/reassembly of the pistol is a bit of a headache. Remove the magazine and empty it; reinsert the magazine; cycle the pistol to be sure it's empty; pull the slide open and press the slide disassembly button; pull the trigger to drop the hammer; remove the magazine; push the main spring housing upward and withdraw it to the rear and downward; and pull the slide off the frame toward the rear. Reassembly is a reverse of this procedure but the hammer must not be cocked.

Reassembly of the pistol is more like a Chinese jigsaw puzzle than a simple task.

Specifications

Overall length: 10 inches
(with 6-inch barrel)
Weight (unloaded,
6-inch barrel): 2 lbs.
Barrel length: 6 inches
Magazine capacity: 10

IVER JOHNSON TP.22B/TP.25B

The TP.22 is the .22 LR model of this pistol and the TP.25 is the .25 ACP version. Both are identical except for differences in chambering. The pistol is actually a variation of the Walther TPH (see below), and has an internal safety coupled to the trigger. Along with the hammer drop manual safety, this makes the pistol easy and safe to carry with the manual safety off and the first shot fired double-action.

Unfortunately the TP.22B doesn't function well with CCI Stingers; it generally works well with Remington Yellow Jackets or Federal Hi-Power ammunition. Possibly a good gunsmith could modify the pistol to work reliably with Stingers by replacing the recoil spring. Purchasers of this pistol should test it out to be sure what ammunition works best.

All in all, the TP.22B or the TP.25B look like ideal hide-away pistols. Takedown is identical to the TPH listed below.

Specifications

Overall length: 5.39 inches
Weight (unloaded): 0.94 lbs.
Barrel length: 2.8 inches
Magazine capacity: 7

JENNINGS J-22

The Jennings pistols are similar to the Raven .25 auto because they were, apparently, created by several members of the Jennings family who own the rights to the pistols.

The big plus of the Jennings pistol is its price: it's usually the lowest in its class. That, coupled with the quality, design, and size makes it an ideal hide-away pistol. Of course you should not expect

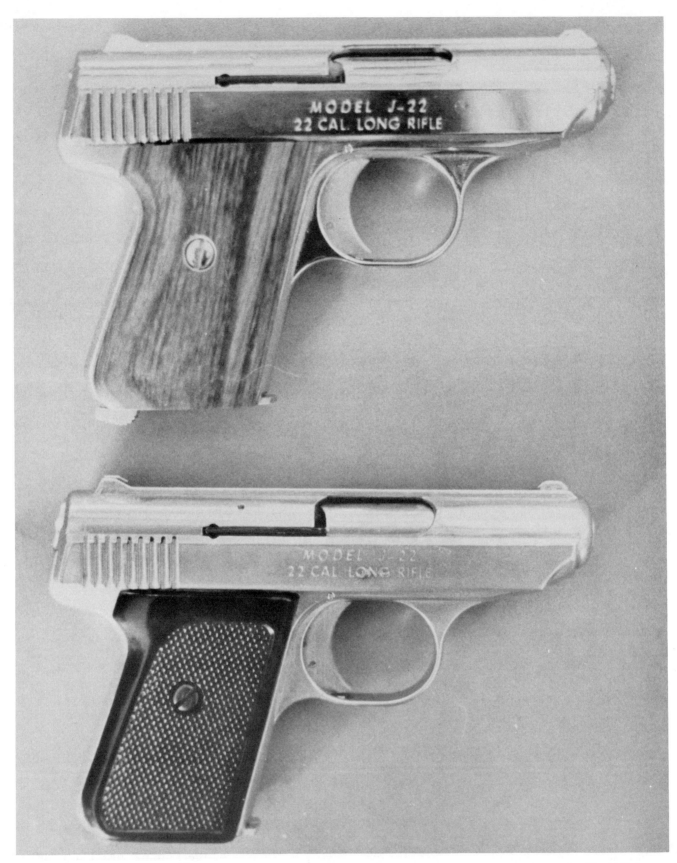

The Jennings J-22 is an ideal hideaway pistol, since it is a good, well-functioning pistol available at a low price. The J-22 has an alloy frame and a steel slide. Sights are minimal and cannot snag on clothing. Three finishes are available with the J-22; shown are the satin nickel (bottom) and the mirror chrome. A tough black Teflon finish is also made. Grip plates are available in walnut or black plastic.

to get the highest quality fit and finish for a low price; the grip fit and machining marks are not quite up to par with guns costing more. But the trade-off is a good, inexpensive, well-functioning pistol.

The J-22 has an alloy frame and a steel slide. Those fired in tests for this book generally preferred CCI Stingers and also worked well with Federal Hi-Power and Remington Vipers. As with most .22 pistols, they often functioned poorly with cheap or low-velocity .22 ammunition.

The pistol has a single-action trigger and a safety located at the forward, top edge of the left grip (it is important to note that the striker cannot be cocked with the safety placed in the "safe" position). The magazine release is located at the grip base. A nice feature is the cocking indicator, a small protrusion that sticks out of the rear of the frame when the striker is locked back. Sights are minimal and should not snag on clothing.

Three finishes are available with the J-22, including satin nickel, mirror chrome, and a tough black Teflon. Grip plates of walnut and black plastic are also available.

Like the Raven, the Jennings pistol is based on many of the Walther Model 9 pistol's features with its striker-retainer/spring catch. This device greatly simplifies manufacture and takedown. All in all, the J-22 is worth considering as a hide-away pistol.

All that has to be done for disassembly is to remove the magazine and cycle the pistol to be sure it's empty; pull the trigger to release the striker; depress the retainer at the rear of the slide

by pushing the retainer in with the rubber eraser on a pencil; lift up the slide at the rear and ease it forward; ease out the retainer (careful; it's spring loaded by the striker); ease out the striker spring; and run the slide forward off the frame. Reassembly is a reversal of this procedure.

Specifications

Overall length: 4.94 inches
Weight (unloaded): 0.82 lbs.
Barrel length: 2.5 inches
Magazine capacity: 6

RAVEN MP25

The Raven .25 auto is a sister gun to the Jennings J-22, and like the J-22, is very inexpensive compared to similar pistols. The price, good design, and size make the Raven a very popular choice in its class. The trade-off is a bit of roughness in fit and finish.

The principle difference between the Raven and J-22 is that the Raven is more squared-off and its extractor is located at the top of the slide rather than the side. The Raven pistol is occasionally finicky about ammunition but generally works well with all types.

The Raven has an alloy frame and a steel slide, a single-action trigger, and a safety located at the forward top edge of the left grip. The striker cannot be cocked with the safety on safe. The magazine release is located at the base of the grip and a cock-

The Raven pistol, in .25 ACP, has a single-action trigger and a safety that is located at the forward, top edge of the left grip. The magazine release is located at the base of the grip. Shown is the tough satin nickel finish with walnut grip plates. Photo courtesy of Raven Arms.

The Raven pistol with chrome finish and "ivory" grip plates. This small .25 ACP pistol is inexpensive but quite well designed. Photo courtesy of Raven Arms.

ing indicator is located on the back of the takedown insert (in the form of a small protrusion that sticks out of the rear hole in the insert). Sights are minimal and will not snag on clothing. Two finishes are available, tough satin nickel and blued steel. Grip plates are of walnut.

The Raven is worth considering as a hide-away pistol. Disassembly is identical to that of the Jennings J-22.

Specifications

Overall length: 4.94 inches
Weight (unloaded): 0.82 lbs.
Barrel length: 2.5 inches
Magazine capacity: 6

RUGER MARK I/II

The Ruger Standard .22 pistol was introduced in 1949 and was practically an instant success. The little pistol had good inherent accuracy, the look of exotic guns like the Luger and Nambu, and a low price tag. It couldn't miss in the marketplace. The original company was created by Alexander Sturm and William B. Ruger who designed the pistol. With the death of Sturm in 1951, the original "Red Eagle" trademark designed by Sturm was changed from red to black.

By 1950, a target version, the Mark I, was marketed. The target model is identical to the Standard except for an adjustable rear sight and two barrel lengths of 5-1/2 and 6-7/8 inches. Later a 5-1/2

inch bull (untapered) barrel was added. Because the pistol uses a bolt inside the receiver, the sights don't move during recoil, allowing the sight picture to come into place more quickly than with slide-mounted sights.

The Ruger's relatively low price is possible because Bill Ruger designed the pistol with an eye toward inexpensive production techniques and functional efficiency. That he was able to create such a weapon that is both beautiful and easy to manufacture is a mark of genius. The frame appears to be milled. Not so. It is made in two halves which are pressed and stamped into shape before being welded into one unit. Steel stampings are also widely used to keep the price of the pistol down.

After extensive testing during the 1970s, the U.S. military discovered that the Ruger pistols were more dependable than the High Standard or other similar .22s. Thus the Ruger often ended up being equipped with silencers and used in the Vietnam War to root out Vietcong in tunnels.

The Ruger is now the most common silenced target-grade .22 pistol. Jonathon Arthur Ciener, Inc., is probably the best known silencer maker for the Mark I and II. For more information on silencer use, see *Silencers in the 1980s* or *Silencers for Hand Firearms,* both available from Paladin Press.

In 1982 a "Mark II" version was introduced with a number of very useful improvements over the Mark I, including an improved trigger system, a bolt stop/slide release, a modified safety which permits placing the weapon on "safe" before

After extensive testing during the 1970s, a number of military suppliers and the U.S. military discovered that Ruger pistols were more dependable than the High Standard or other similar .22s. The U.S. government continues to purchase pistols from Ruger. Note the "U.S." stamp on the receiver of this Ruger Mark II. Photo courtesy of Sturm, Ruger & Company, Inc.

By 1979, one million Ruger Mark I pistols had been produced. In 1982 a Mark II version (shown here) was introduced. Among the improvements incorporated into the new pistol is an improved trigger system, a bolt stop/slide release, modified safety (which permits placing the weapon on safe before cocking it), and a milled area in the receiver next to the charging slide. Photo courtesy of Sturm, Ruger & Company, Inc.

Left view of the current U.S. military model of the Ruger Mark II pistol. Note bull barrel and target sights. Photo courtesy of Sturm, Ruger & Company, Inc.

Following the Vietnam War, several companies started to offer silenced versions of the Ruger pistols. While this pistol appears to be a bull-barrel version, a suppressor is actually wrapped around the normal-diameter barrel. Jonathon Arthur Ciener, Inc., is probably the best known company currently making silencers for the Mark Is and IIs. Photo courtesy of Jonathon Arthur Ciener.

cocking it, and a milled area next to the charging slide. For general shooting, the Mark II is the best bet; Mark Is are probably best left to collectors.

The Mark II is currently available in a number of versions: the Standard model with a 4-3/4- and 6-inch barrel; the Target with a 6-7/8-inch barrel as well as a bull barrel target model with 5-1/2-inch and 10-inch barrel lengths. All are available in either blued or stainless steel.

There are two real pluses to the Ruger pistols: they are tough and they are reliable with a wide range of ammunition. The target models are also very accurate, considering the inexpensive price tag; many target shooters using quality ammunition are able to average 1-inch groups at 25 yards. More importantly for combat purposes, high-velocity ammunition will normally expand the group size by only 1/4-inch at 25 yards.

Given the accuracy of the Ruger pistols, a scope sight might be considered for some purposes. An excellent mount is available from Brownells for both the Mark I and II. The mount is made by B-Square and retails for $50; it can be used with any 1-inch scope.

Since the Ruger's grip angle is similar to that of the Browning Hi-Power, Beretta 92, Colt 1911-A1, and many other larger combat pistols, you can use the Ruger to build up marksmanship skills with the other pistols, especially with Clark "45"

adapter grips. The Clark grips have the basic shape and angle of the 1911-A1 and can readily simulate other grips. They are available from Brownells for $20.

The Ruger pistols do present some potential problems, all of which can be overcome. One is the lack of a side-of-the-grip magazine release. The Ruger magazine release is at the base of the grip, and works well but is far from ideal for quick reloading. There are two after-market solutions. One is the replacement nylon release made by Ram Line; it extends from the base of the grip farther so that it is more easily operated. The other is Red-E Products' "Thumb Activated Magazine Release" which provides a side-mounted release on the left grip. This unit goes into place and slides along the side cut inside the left grip; it extends down to rotate the replacement magazine release mounted in the base of the grip. (Though the action needed to make it function is downward rather than pressing on a button, the two are very similar and it seems second nature to those used to button magazine releases. While this seems like a major undertaking, it is only a matter of taking the grips off, replacing the base release, and making a small cut in the left grip with a pocket knife or similar tool. Care must be taken to place the washers that come with the kit under the bottom left grip screw or to grind off the screw so that it

The Mark II comes in a number of versions, including this stainless-steel standard version with 6-inch barrel. Photo courtesy of Sturm, Ruger & Company, Inc.

The Ruger Mark II Target pistol is available in a low-maintenance, stainless-steel version with 6 7/8-inch barrel. Photo courtesy of Sturm, Ruger & Company, Inc.

doesn't cause the release to malfunction. The only snag which was encountered during testing the Red-E release was that the spring in the grip of the test Mark II was a little short; a quick squeeze with needle-nose pliers extended it without problem and everything worked fine. The release seemed a little long, too, so about a fourth of an inch was ground off its top.)

The Ruger magazines are another source of minor irritation. They are hard to reload. Ram Line has come out with a plastic magazine for the Mark I/II. On the Mark II the magazine holds the slide open after the last round is fired, just like the Ruger magazines, and best of all, it is easy to load and holds two extra rounds. Ram Line magazines are a must for a Mark I or II.

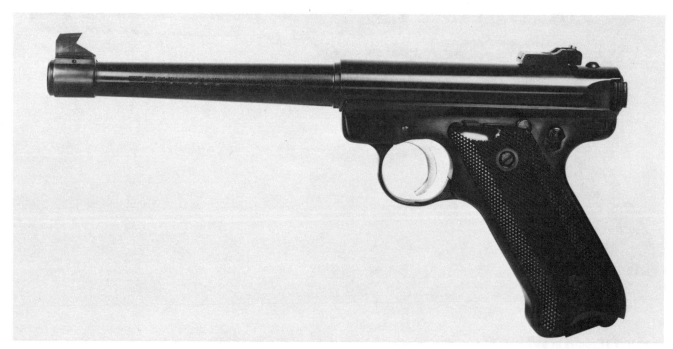

The Ruger Mark II Target model pistol in its 6 7/8-inch barrel, blued form. Photo courtesy of Sturm, Ruger & Company, Inc.

The Ruger Mark II Bull-Barrel version with a 10-inch barrel gives bullets fired from it nearly as much velocity—or perhaps as much velocity—as can be obtained with a .22 rifle. The heavy barrel is sometimes mistaken for a silenced weapon. Shown is the stainless-steel model. Photo courtesy of Sturm, Ruger & Company, Inc.

The Ruger pistols are tedious to field-strip when compared to many other 22s. Reassembly is even harder than the takedown. Ideally both are carried out with a rubber or rawhide mallet at your side.

Here's the disassembly procedure (use the owner's manual to locate various parts): remove the magazine and cycle the pistol to be sure it's empty, then release the bolt; pull the trigger to be sure the hammer is down; use a small screwdriver or pocket knife to release the housing latch in the pistol grip; swing the mainspring housing out and pull the bolt stop pin out of the receiver; hit the rear of the bolt/receiver with a soft mallet to knock the receiver/barrel unit off the frame; and remove the bolt assembly from the barrel and receiver. This will allow you to clean the pistol fully; further disassembly is not recommended.

Reassembly is basically a reversal of the above procedure, but there are a few tricks. First, be sure the hammer is forward, not cocked back. Second,

The Ruger Mark II Bull-Barrel version has target sights and a heavy barrel that is ideal for developing wrist muscles for shooting large-caliber pistols. This model of the pistol has a 5½-inch barrel and blued steel finish. Photo courtesy of Sturm, Ruger & Company, Inc.

The Clark "45" adapter grips for the Ruger Mark I/II pistols allow you to quickly and easily change the grip angle of the Ruger to that of the Browning, Colt, or Beretta 92 pistols. The Clark grips have the basic shape and angle of the 1911-A1 and can be readily modified with a little do-it-yourself work to simulate a number of other grips as well. The grip is available from Brownells and makes a worthwhile modification to the pistol. Photo courtesy of Brownells.

be sure the hammer strut sticks down into the well in the forward side of the mainspring housing. To reassemble, slide the bolt into the rear of the barrel/receiver unit, being careful the right side is up; place the hammer forward; place the receiver/ barrel unit on the frame and push it backward (you will probably need to hit the barrel lightly with the mallet to drive it home); place the mainspring's bolt stop pin into the base of the receiver and into the barrel; pull back on the trigger and let the hammer fall forward; be sure that the hammer strut is resting in the mainspring well as the unit is latched shut (if you fail to do this, the unit won't go together or the bolt won't cock after the pistol is assembled); push the main spring latch into place; lock the housing latch; and pull the bolt to be sure everything is functioning correctly. Get a cold drink and sit down to congratulate yourself on a job well done!

Once you get the hang of assembling and disassembling the Ruger pistol, you'll find it isn't so hard, but the first few times are wild. Nevertheless, nearly everyone who owns a Mark I or II has found it worth the trouble to have such a fine pistol. The disassembly hassle has a nice trade-off: it's possible to change the barrel assembly easily and have several barrel lengths and styles to go on one frame. This allows you to create custom pistols to suit different needs.

All in all, the Mark I and II pistols are ideal for training, covert, target, or other uses, and are the first choice in their size/use group.

Specifications of Ruger Mark II Standard (short barrel)

Overall length: 8.31 inches
Weight (unloaded): 2.25 lbs.
Barrel length: 4.75 inches
(6-inch, long barrel version)
Magazine capacity: 10

Specifications of Ruger Mark II Target

Overall length: 11.13 inches
Weight (unloaded): 2.63 lbs.
Barrel length: 6.88 inches
Magazine capacity: 10

Specifications of Ruger Mark II Bull Barrel

Overall length: 9.06 inches
(13.56 inches long barrel)
Weight (unloaded): 2.63 lbs.
(3.25 lbs. long barrel)
Barrel length: 5.5 inches
(10 inches long barrel)
Magazine capacity: 10

SEECAMP

The Seecamp pistol was originally chambered for .25 ACP but has been rechambered for the .32 ACP Winchester Silverpoint. Because its size remains the same with the larger cartridge, the .32 pistol is a better choice for self-defense. See the section on .32/.380 pistols for more information.

SIG-SAUER P-230

This pistol is available in a number of more potent chamberings besides .22 LR. Since the size is the same for all the different chamberings, it would be wise to relegate the .22 model to practice. For more information, see the chapter on .32/.380 pistols.

SMITH & WESSON M41

This single-action target pistol, introduced in 1951, is well made and known for its accuracy. Its grip shape is more compatible with other larger automatics and has a button magazine release on its left side. The squared-off barrel makes the use of a silencer nearly impossible, but the pistol might be an alternate choice to the Ruger Mark II—though the M41 carries a premium price. A heavy-barrel version is also available and a stripped budget version is sometimes to be found as the Model 46.

Specifications

Overall length: 12 inches
Weight (unloaded): 2.72 lbs.
Barrel length: 7.38 inches
Magazine capacity: 10

STEEL CITY DOUBLE DEUCE

This is an American-made model of the Walther TPH and has little to distinguish it from other Walther copies except for an ambidextrous safety. The pistol comes with rosewood grips and is available in both .22 LR and .25 ACP.

STERLING 300/302

Although the Sterling Arms Company is now

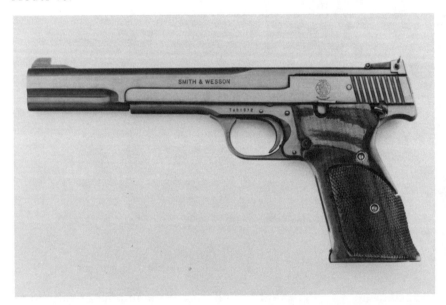

A heavy-barrel version of the M41 is available. The barrel is only 5½ inches long, which makes it similar to many other combat automatics in larger calibers. Photo courtesy of Smith & Wesson.

The S&W M41 is a single-action target pistol first introduced by Smith & Wesson in 1951. It is well made and known for its accuracy. The pistol has a grip shape more compatible with that of other larger automatics and has a button magazine release located on the left side of the pistol grip. Shown is the 7-inch-barreled standard version. Photo courtesy of Smith & Wesson.

The Sterling Arms Model 302 (chambered for .22 LR) is no longer made, but often turns up in the used gun market. The pistols aren't bad, but are not nearly as good as the Jennings J-22.

out of business, the small 300 (.25 ACP) and 302 (.22 LR) pistols are often found for sale. They are about the same size as the Jennings J-22 but are not nearly as tough or convenient to take down. The Jennings J-22 or the Raven would be a better choice.

STOEGER LUGER 22

A .22 LR copy of the Luger. It has little to offer that is not found on other better pistols.

TITAN PISTOLS

These are cheap blowback pistols made in Italy and chambered for low-power rounds like .22 LR, .32 ACP, and .380 ACP. They have some good design features but often aren't well finished or dependable. For combat purposes, it would be best to get a different type of pistol.

WALTHER PP, PPK, PPK/S

The Walther PP has a huge number of variations. Some are chambered for the .22 LR and .25 ACP, although the .32 and .380 are the most common chamberings. The .22 version of the pistol would be a good practice weapon, but because the .22 and .25 pistols are the same size as the larger PP/PPKs, it is probably a better bet to go with the more potent chamberings or with a smaller .22 pistol like the Walther TPH, Jennings J-22, etc. For more information on the Walther PP, see the section on .32/.380 pistols.

One version of the Walther PP which might be of interest as a covert or target weapon is the Manurhin PP Sport. It has a very accurate 6- or 7-5/8-inch barrel and an extended magazine and grip. The hammer has a spur, and target sights take advantage of the pistol's inherent accuracy. Of special interest to those needing a silenced weapon is the fact that the front sight is mounted with a threaded nut. For covert actions this pistol should be considered, especially if the user is already familiar with the Walther PP series of weapons.

WALTHER TPH

The TPH is often called a scaled-down Walther PP. In fact, it can be traced back to the Walther Model 9 and TP pistols.

The TP was created from the Model 9 in 1961 and chambered for both .25 ACP and .22 LR. The pistol had a finger rest on the magazine bottom plate and a slide-mounted safety which locked the striker. It was discontinued in 1971 with the introduction of the TPH.

The TPH is small. Too small, according to the 1968 Gun Control Act, which banned the importation of the pistol except for law-enforcement use. The pistol was an immediate success in Europe, however, and continues to be manufactured there in large numbers.

In 1978, work was started under the direction of Interarms at the Ranger Manufacturing Plant in Gadsen, Alabama, on a licensed copy of the PPK/S chambered in .380 ACP. Once the company was established, Interarms/Ranger Manufacturing started tooling up for production of the PPK and TPH. Due to a loophole in the GCA, these two guns can be legally sold in the United States if they are built here, so the TPH is now available in the United States.

The TPH operates by straight blowback; its barrel is permanently mounted to the frame, where it serves as the guide rod for the recoil spring.

The thumb safety is mounted on the slide and consists of a lever which locks the firing pin and blocks it from the hammer as well as dropping the hammer when engaged. A frame-mounted internal safety also blocks the firing pin from the hammer unless the trigger is pulled back; this allows the TPH to be carried with the slide safety in the "fire" position and a round in the chamber. This feature, coupled with the double-action trigger, makes the TPH an ideal pocket pistol. The magazine release is at the base of the pistol grip.

The TPH pistols built by Interarms are available in blued and stainless steel, as well as with a lightweight aluminum frame.

Field-stripping is quite simple and similar to the PPK: cycle the action to be sure it is empty; pull down on the trigger guard to release the slide block; pull the slide back and lift the rear of it clear off the frame; and push the slide forward off the barrel. Reassembly is basically a reversal of this procedure.

Specifications (steel frame)

Overall length: 5.3 inches
Weight (unloaded): 0.94 lbs.
Barrel length: 2.75 inches
Magazine capacity: 6

WILKINSON ARMS "SHERRY"

This is a small, simple .22 LR automatic with an awkward cross-bolt safety located in the rear of the frame. It is an attractive-looking pistol but has little to offer that can't be found in less expensive pistols like the Jennings J-22.

.32 ACP and .380 ACP

Most .32 ACP pistols are nearly identical to their .380 counterparts. Given the better ballistics of the .380 cartridge, it is usually wise to go with the more potent round. The .32 continues to be popular in Europe, but it is probable the twenty-first century will see the demise of the .32 ACP.

New bullet configurations give the .380 more wallop than it used to have. While it is still less potent than the .38 Special in most loadings, it can approach, and, with wise selection of ammunition, can even surpass the FMJ loads that some still insist on carrying in revolvers.

For best effectiveness, the Glaser Safety Slug makes a lot of sense provided it will function well in the pistol. More reliable and easier on the pocketbook are the more common Winchester Silvertips or similar ammunition from other major manufacturers.

Probably the best automatic pistols in the .32/.380 category are the various Beretta models and the Walther PP variants, though many others (such as the H&K 4, H&K P7-K3, and Charter Arms 79K) may be more suitable for some individuals.

AMERICAN ARMS EAGLE

This pistol is a Walther PPK variation. Chambered for the .380 ACP, it is made in the U.S. by Wilkerson Firearms and was first introduced in 1984. It has little to offer that can't be found with a genuine PP or PPK. See the Walther PP/PPK section for specifications and field-stripping information.

AMT BACKUP

This pistol is also available in .22 LR. The pistol has a concealed hammer. Unfortunately, the manual safety is placed where one would expect to find a magazine-release button, while the magazine release is located at the grip base. Things are somewhat redeemed with a heavy trigger pull and a grip safety which might allow one to carry the pistol with the manual safety in the "fire" position.

Field-stripping is complicated and requires an Allen wrench and other tools. The heavy trigger pull adversely affects accuracy. As with the .22 model, the magazine finger rest might be removed to aid in concealability. All in all, this is probably not the best choice for a hide-away gun.

Specifications

Overall length: 4.25 inches
Weight (unloaded): 18 oz.
Barrel length: 2.5 inches
Magazine capacity: 5 (8 rounds in .22 LR)

ASTRA CONSTABLE

This pistol is available in .22 LR as well as .380 ACP. It is loosely designed around the Walther PP with a double-action trigger and internal firing-pin safety; the principle difference is in the Constable's disassembly lever on the frame inside the trigger guard. The magazine release is also located in a more convenient position than that of the PP,

and a slide release is found just above the magazine release. Disassembly is nearly identical to the Walther PP except for the disassembly button.

While the pistol's design is good, the Constable has a rather poor reputation for reliability.

Specifications

Overall length: 6.69 inches
Weight (unloaded): 1.5 lbs.
Barrel length: 3.5 inches
Magazine capacity: 7 (10 rounds in .22 LR)

BERETTA MODEL 1934

The Models 1931 and 1934 are upgraded variations of the Model 1915 which Tullio Marengoni created for the Italian military. The 1931 was adopted by the Italian Navy; it has a straight backstrap and a tendency to point low. The Army adopted the 1934; this model has a curved

The Beretta 1934, chambered in .380 ACP, and the somewhat rarer "1935" (shown), chambered in .32 ACP, saw action in Italy's Ethiopian campaign and in the Spanish Civil War. Though chambered for low-power rounds, the pistol functioned reliably on the battlefield and thus remained the standard Italian service pistol until 1951.

backstrap which offers better pointing. Both are chambered for the .380. Limited numbers of the 1934 which were manufactured in .32 ACP for the Italian Navy and Air Force are sometimes referred to as the "Model 1935." The 1934 saw action in Italy's Ethiopian campaign and in the Spanish Civil War. Though chambered for low-power rounds, the pistols functioned reliably on the battlefield and remained the standard Italian service pistol until 1951.

Following World War II, Beretta exported the 1934 to the United States as the Cougar in .380 ACP and the Puma in .32 ACP. In 1958 Beretta discontinued the 1934/1935; it is estimated that 500,000 of the pistols were made in .380 ACP and 600,000 in .32 ACP.

The slides of the various models have the Beretta look, a cut-out in the top of the slide which leaves the barrel exposed. This cut-out also simplifies disassembly, reduces weight, and makes an empty cartridge less apt to jam in the slide during extraction. The magazine has a hook to support the little finger and aid magazine change. The magazine release is located on the bottom of the pistol grip.

The safety allows the weapon to be easily field-stripped, but its placement is very awkward. Consequently, people who carry this pistol for combat often leave the safety in the "fire" position with the hammer (perhaps in the half-cocked position) over a chambered round. Carrying a pistol in this manner is dangerous, however, since dropping the pistol on its hammer may cause a discharge; it's just that, in combat, fumbling with the safety is more dangerous.

A .22 LR version of the 1935 was also made by Beretta and known as the 948. The 948 is nearly identical to the .32/.380 version but lacks a half-cock notch in its hammer. This, coupled with the lack of an inertial firing pin, makes it extremely dangerous to carry the pistol with the safety off and a round in the chamber. Several long-barreled versions of the 948 were also offered. One was a dual-barreled kit gun (with a standard and a 6-inch barrel); the other, the 949 target pistol.

Takedown is simple. Remove the magazine; pull the slide back and make sure the weapon is empty; push the safety up in the notch in the slide so that it is locked open; tap the muzzle of the barrel with the hand; remove the barrel through the top receiver slot; and disengage the safety so that the slide can be removed by allowing it to travel off the front of the weapon. Reassembly is a reversal of this procedure.

The 1931/1934/1935 Berettas are not noted for accuracy. This may be due in part to their heavy trigger action and brutal recoil created by the guns' light weight. The pistols are noted for their strength and reliability, however, and were very well liked by the Italian servicemen who carried them.

The 1931/1934/1935 Berettas are not noted for their accuracy, but are instead noted for their strength and reliability. These pistols are very well liked by those who carry, or who have carried them, for self-defense.

Specifications

Overall length: 6 inches
Weight (unloaded): 1.25 lbs.
Barrel length: 3.5 inches
Barrel twist: 4 grooves, right-hand
Magazine capacity: 7 (8 rounds in .32 ACP)

BERETTA SERIES 70 PISTOLS

In 1958, when Beretta discontinued its 1934-style pistols in .32, .380, and .22 LR, a new series of pistols was introduced, consisting of the Model 70 in .32 ACP (exported as the "New Puma"), Model 71 in .22 LR (exported as the "Jaguar"), Model 72 in .22 LR with two barrels of different length, Model 73 in .22 LR with a longer grip frame/magazine and a long target barrel, Model 72 in .22 LR with long barrel and adjustable sights, and Model 75, which was similar to the 72 but had only one barrel. Later, Model 76 was added which was a full-fledged target pistol with extended frame and optional wooden contoured grips. (To make things confusing, a 100 series of the identical pistols was marketed with some of the identical 70 series models. The Model 71 became the 101, Model 76 was the 102, and the Model 1951 9mm Luger became the 104. These designations were apparently soon abandoned by Beretta so that they are not often seen anymore.)

The firing mechanism of these pistols is that of the Beretta Model 1951. All the series 70 pistols are blessed with an easy-to-use takedown lever on the right side of the frame. Early Model 70s had a cross-bolt safety; this was later replaced with a much more desirable frame-mounted thumb lever. During the late 1970s, a magazine disconnect safety was added to the pistols (these have an "S" suffix on their model designation); some users may wish to remove this safety so that the pistol can be fired while changing magazines.

Newer models of the Beretta 70 have all been lumped into the "70S" designation, along with a .380 chambering in addition to the .32 and .22 LR versions. Thus, all the models became the 70S with the only difference being the chambering, except for the target pistol version which remained the 76S.

Disassembly is nearly identical to that of the Beretta Model 84 below.

Specifications of 70S, .32 ACP

Overall length: 6.5 inches
Weight (unloaded): 1.44 lbs.
Barrel length: 3.5 inches
Magazine capacity: 8

Specifications of 70S, .380 ACP

Overall length: 6.5 inches
Weight (unloaded): 1.44 lbs.
Barrel length: 3.5 inches
Magazine capacity: 7

Specifications of 70S, .22 LR

Overall length: 6.5 inches
Weight (unloaded): 1.13 lbs.
Barrel length: 3.5 inches
Magazine capacity: 8

BERETTA MODEL 90

This pistol looks more like a Walther PP than a Beretta. (It's one of the few Berettas not having the distinctive slide cut-out over the barrel that has become the Beretta trademark.) The pistol was designed in the mid-1960s and introduced for sale in 1968 chambered for the .32 ACP.

The pistol has a thumb safety on the frame and a magazine release on the left side of the pistol grip behind the trigger guard. It also has a double-action trigger—another first for a Beretta. The hammer is exposed so that the weapon can be cocked for single-action fire on the first shot. A few of the pistols were made with a slide release lever.

This pistol was discontinued in 1982 and replaced by the 81/84 series. All in all, the pistol offers little that can't be found in other automatics.

BERETTA 81/84 SERIES

In 1975 Beretta introduced a new family of pistols. The .32 ACP version was designated the Model 81; in .380 ACP, the Model 84. Both pistols have double-row magazines, takedown levers on the right side of the frame, reversible magazine release buttons on the pistol grip just behind the trigger guard, slide release levers, and a convenient ambidextrous frame safety. Beretta designers again included their traditional slide cut-out over the barrel of the pistol.

The pistols can be carried cocked and locked for a quick single- or double-action first shot using the frame safety. There is no automatic firing-pin block, so it is rather risky to carry the pistol with the hammer down and the safety off over a loaded chamber. A loaded chamber indicator is created with a red section of the extractor. The pistols are also blessed with the dubious magazine disconnector safety. The pistols have large grips which make them look awkward. In fact, the large grip makes a very comfortable good pointing firearm.

In the mid-1980s, two new versions were added with single-column magazines. The .32 ACP is the Model 82 and the .380 ACP is the Model 85. Late models have grooves on the front and back of the grip straps and are also offered in a "BB" model. The 81/82/84/85 BB models have a firing-pin block coupled with the trigger so that the pistol can be carried with the safety off and fired double-action on the first shot. A nickel finish is also available with these models, and a "W" suffix is used for walnut grips and "P" for plastic.

Beretta also makes a modified version of the 84 for Browning which doesn't have the slide cut-out on the top and does have a hammer spur and a slide-mounted, ambidextrous safety. It is marketed in the U.S. by Browning as the BDA .380 Auto and by FN in Belgium as the Model 140.

Recently, 86 and 87BB pistols have been created. The 86 is a .380 pistol much like the 84/85, but has a tip-up barrel like that of many of Beretta's .22 LR and .25 ACP pistols; while this feature might be ideal for a handicapped shooter, it is not good for combat because of the extra steps needed due to the lack of an extractor to load a round into the chamber if the pistol misfires. The 81/82 and 84/85 pistols are better for combat use.

The 87BB is chambered for .22 LR. This completes a family of quality pistols which are similar in function and pointability to many of the Beretta 92 9mm Luger series. Like other Beretta pistols, the 80 series is noted for reliability and quality of fit and assembly.

Field-stripping any of the 80 series Berettas is quite simple. Remove the magazine and cycle the pistol to be sure it's empty; rotate the disassembly lever downward; push the slide off the frame; carefully push the recoil spring and rod toward the front of the slide to release it and lift the spring and rod out; and remove the barrel. Reassembly is a reverse of this procedure.

Specifications for 81 (.32 ACP)

Overall length: 6.8 inches
Weight (unloaded): 1.47 lbs.
Barrel length: 3.82 inches
Magazine capacity: 12

In 1975 Beretta introduced a new family of pistols including this Model 84 chambered for .380 ACP. The pistols have double-row magazines, takedown levers, and reversible magazine release buttons. The pistols can be carried "cocked and locked" for a quick single-action first shot using the frame safety, or with the first shot fired double-action.

Specifications for 82 (.32 ACP)

Overall length: 6.8 inches
Weight (unloaded): 1.06 lbs.
Barrel length: 3.82 inches
Magazine capacity: 9

Specifications for 84 (.380 ACP)

Overall length: 6.8 inches
Weight (unloaded): 1.4 lbs (1.06 lbs., "BB")
Barrel length: 3.82 inches
Magazine capacity: 13

Specifications for 85 (.380 ACP)

Overall length: 6.8 inches
Weight (unloaded): 1.06 lbs.
Barrel length: 3.82 inches
Magazine capacity: 8

Specifications for 87 (.22 LR)

Overall length: 6.8 inches
Weight (unloaded): 1.25 lbs.
Barrel length: 3.82 inches
Magazine capacity: 10

BERNARDELLI P018

According to company literature, the .32 ACP P018 is nearly identical to the 9mm Luger double-action model pistol and "the hammer forged barrels are interchangeable, affording the luxury of owning two pistols in one." Whether or not this is actually possible remains to be seen as the pistols become available in the United States.

The P018 is milled from steel and available in a number of finishes and in a standard and chopped model. These pistols promise a lot and it is hoped they will deliver on their promises.

BERNARDELLI USA

The USA is based on the Walther PPK and is available in .22 LR as well as .32 and .380. It comes with a click-adjustable rear sight. (At the time of this writing, the pistol was unavailable and is new enough not to have built up either a good or bad reputation.)

BERSA 383

The Bersa Model 383 is an Argentinian version of the Walther PP. About the only major change

The Browning BDA is actually made by Beretta; the pistol is nearly identical to the Beretta Model 84, except that it doesn't have the barrel cutout and does have a hammer spur and slide-mounted hammer block ambidextrous safety. The modified Beretta is marketed in the United States by Browning as the "BDA .380 Auto" and by FN in Belgium as the "Model 140." Photo courtesy of Browning Firearms.

is a thumb rest on the grip, an up-to-date hooked trigger guard, and a takedown lever. Unfortunately, the firing-pin block seems to have been left off, so that it is not all that safe to carry with the hammer down and the safety off. For a hide-away gun, this is not the first choice.

BROWNING BDA

The Browning BDA is actually made in Italy by Beretta and marketed by Browning. The pistol is nearly identical to the Beretta Model 84 except that it doesn't have the barrel cut-out on the top of the slide and does have a hammer spur and a slide-mounted hammer block ambidextrous safety. The modified Beretta is also marketed in the United States by Browning as the BDA .380 Auto and by FN in Belgium as the Model 140. Takedown and specifications are nearly identical to those of the 84. The pistol is well made and makes a good companion pistol to the new Browning double-action Hi-Power in 9mm Luger.

CHARTER ARMS MODEL 79K

The 79K is made in Germany (apparently by Erma-Werke) and imported by Charter Arms. Although the pistol looks like a Browning-style design, it is in actuality similar to the Walther PP. When the pistol is disassembled, what looks like the recoil spring guide and the barrel bushing is actually a molded section of the slide. The recoil spring is really around the barrel.

There are several nice changes in the design. The 79K has a slide-mounted safety which doesn't drop the hammer, so the weapon can be carried cocked and locked, with the hammer down on a loaded round with the safety off; the gun can then be fired double-action for the first shot.

About the only drawback to this pistol is that its magazine release is located on the pistol grip base. However, because of the single-column magazine, the pistol is quite thin and can be used as a backup or hide-away pistol.

The 79K is available in .32 ACP or .380 ACP in

Charter Arms Model 79K looks like a Browning-style design, but is actually similar to the Walther PP pistols. The 79K makes an ideal "hideout" pistol, thanks to its thin design and double-action trigger.

stainless steel with a satin finish and walnut grip plates. Smaller but nearly identical is the Charter Arms Model 40 chambered for .22 LR. In addition to being useful as hide-away pistols, the two Charter Arms guns also operate similarly to a S&W or Browning automatic.

Field-stripping is identical to the Walther PP.

Specifications for 79K

Overall length: 6.5 inches
Weight (unloaded): 1.53 lbs.
Barrel length: 3.6 inches
Magazine capacity: 7

Specifications for Model 40

Overall length: 6.3 inches
Weight (unloaded): 1.34 lbs.
Barrel length: 3.3 inches
Magazine capacity: 7

COLT MUSTANG

The Mustang is more or less a chopped version of the Colt 380 Government pistol (see below). It is nearly as small as many .22 LR or .25 ACP pistols, and as such, is an ideal hide-away pistol with greater "umph" than .22 LR/.25 ACP weapons.

Currently the Mustang is only available in a black oxide finish, but a nickel or stainless/anodized mode may become available if the pistol is successful.

Like the .380, the Mustang fires from a locked

breech. This lowers felt recoil considerably and allows the use of "hot" commercial loads. The pistol also uses nestled double recoil springs which greatly aid in reducing recoil. A barrel with an oversized outer diameter at the muzzle does away with the barrel bushing.

Field-stripping is quite simple. Remove the magazine and cycle the pistol to be sure it's empty; pull the slide back to its disassembly notch and push out the slide release lever from right to left; remove the slide off the front of the frame; carefully push the recoil spring and rod toward the front of the slide to release, and lift the spring and rod out; and remove the barrel. Reassembly is the reverse of this procedure, but take care not to press down on the spring-loaded ejector, as it can become locked into the top of the sear spring. Should this happen, remove the grip panels and turn the pistol upside down so that a screwdriver can reach through the magazine well and free the ejector. When reassembling the recoil springs and guide, take care not to leave out their washer; they should go into the slide before the barrel.

Specifications

Overall length: 5.6 inches
Weight (unloaded): 1.16 lbs.
Barrel length: 2.73 inches
Magazine capacity: 5

COLT 380 GOVERNMENT MODEL

The 380 Government Model is a small .380 ACP pistol modeled after Colt's 1911-A1 .45.

The 380 Government Model is a small .380 ACP pistol modeled on Colt's 1911-A1 .45 pistol. The safety, magazine release, and slide release are all located in identical positions as on the Colt, making this pistol ideal as a backup piece. Photo courtesy of Colt Firearms.

Similar to the .32 ACP created for the U.S. military for issue to general officers and security personnel during WWII, the 380 Government Model is chambered .380 ACP and is available in nickel finish (shown) or blued metal. Photo courtesy of Colt Firearms.

Placement of safety, magazine release, and slide release are all identical, making the 380 an ideal backup weapon.

A pistol similar to the 380 was originally created in .32 ACP for the U.S. military during World War II for issue to general officers and security personnel. Like many Colt firearms, these found their way to the commercial marketplace.

The MK IV Series 80 models are available in blued metal, satin nickel finish, and bright nickel finish with a white grip. The satin finished pistol is probably best for hide-away use due to its corrosion resistance. Unfortunately, early 380s exhibited a rather poor quality finish and trigger pull; newer pistols are of higher quality and should be purchased when possible. Most 380 pistols need a throating job in order to chamber hollowpoint ammunition reliably.

Field-stripping is similar to the 1911-A1 and the Mustang. Be careful not to depress the ejector too far when putting the slide back onto the frame, as the ejector will lock down into the frame where it can only be removed with a screwdriver or similar tool with great effort.

Specifications

Overall length: 6.13 inches
Weight (unloaded): 1.36 lbs.
Barrel length: 3.25 inches
Magazine capacity: 7

CONCORDE PMK 380

This is yet another Walther PP variation. It has little to offer that isn't found on the original design.

CZ-83

This Czechoslovakian pistol is chambered in .32 (used by the police and many paramilitary groups in Europe) and .380 ACP; the latter is a much better combat pistol. The CZ-83 is currently being imported into the United States by Bauska.

An ambidextrous magazine-release button is located at the rear of the trigger guard and the hammer has a spur. A slide-lock release is just above the left grip. The double-action trigger is coupled to an internal safety which allows the pistol to be carried with relative safety with the hammer down and the manual safety off. An ambidextrous safety is mounted on the frame and can only be engaged when the hammer is cocked. This feature prevents inadvertent engagement.

The trigger guard is large so that the pistol may be used with gloves. The rear sight can be drift adjusted for windage, and the grip panels are black plastic. Finish on early pistols is a rough blue with some heavy-wear parts having an aluminum beryllium silicate finish. Newer pistols may have an epoxy paint finish if other Czech firearms are any indication.

Field-stripping is nearly identical to the Walther PP; the main difference is that the trigger guard locks down during disassembly. The firing pin is held in place with a Colt 1911-A1-style removable block.

Because of problems in obtaining the pistol in the United States as well as hard-to-get spare parts, the CZ-83 is probably not the best choice in the .32/.380 class. It is as large as some 9mm Luger pistols which far outclass it in bullet performance.

Specifications

Overall length: 6.8 inches
Weight (unloaded): 1.64 lbs.
Barrel length: 3.8 inches
Magazine capacity: 15 rounds in .32 ACP
13 rounds in .380 ACP

DETONICS POCKET 380

This is one of a family of small, stainless steel hide-away pistols offered by Detonics. It has a slide-mounted thumb safety/firing-pin block, magazine release at the rear of the hooked trigger guard, bobbed hammer, and double-action trigger. The sights are somewhat exposed but rounded to give more or less snag-free use. For information on other models of the Pocket 9 pistol, see the 9mm Luger section.

Specifications

Overall length: 5.75 inches
Weight (unloaded): 1.4 lbs.
Barrel length: 3 inches
Magazine capacity: 6

ERMA KGP38

This pistol is modeled after the Luger (Parabellum) design in .380 ACP. With a long barrel and only a 5-round magazine, it is far from an ideal combat weapon.

The Detonics Pocket 380 is one of the series of small, stainless-steel pistols offered by Detonics that is designed specifically for hideaway use. The sights are somewhat exposed, but rounded to give more or less snagfree use when the pistol is concealed. Photo courtesy of Detonics.

ERMA-WERKE EP 459

This pistol is nearly identical to the Charter Arms K-79. The 459 also has a sister pistol, the EP 452, in .22 LR.

H&K 4

This pistol is based on the old Mauser HSc design. The H&K 4 was used by the German Customs Police for some time as the P11. The weapon is available in .32 ACP and .380 ACP as well as .22 LR and .25 ACP. It has a double-action trigger for a quick first shot and can be safely carried with the safety in the fire position. The safety is mounted on the right side of the slide; the magazine release is on the grip base.

Because it can quickly change from one caliber to another, the H&K 4 makes an ideal kit gun. All that is necessary is to change the barrel, recoil spring, and magazine. (When going from center-fire to .22 LR, it is also necessary to change the breech block face plate by unscrewing it and rotating it halfway around to reposition the firing pin.)

The H&K 4 was imported into the States by Harrington and Richardson from the 1960s until the early 70s when Heckler and Koch set up its own U.S. facility. This pistol may be phased out in order to make room for the new H&K P7-K3, which will be able to use .22 LR, .32 ACP, and .380 ACP. Nevertheless, the H&K 4 should be available for some time; it has the same quality for

which H&K is known.

Specifications

Overall length: 6.17 inches
Weight (unloaded): 1 lb.
Barrel length: 3.35 inches
Magazine capacity: 7 in .380, 8 in other calibers

H&K P7-K3

This pistol is a kit gun with interchangeable barrel/magazine/spring kits that allow it to shoot .22 LR, .32 ACP, or .380 ACP. The pistol is nearly identical to the 9mm version of the P7 described in the chapter on 9mm pistols.

IVER JOHNSON PONY

This is a Browning/Colt style pistol chambered only for .380 ACP. It is more compact than the Colt 380 Government Model and is a viable choice for a .380 1911-style pistol, though the new Colt Mustang may seize much of that market.

The Pony fires from a locked breech; both slide and frame are made of steel. Its thumb safety is frame-mounted and the weapon fires single-action only. The Pony is available with walnut grips and blue ("P0380B" model), nickel ("P0380N"), and parkerized ("P0380M") finishes.

Disassembly is nearly identical to that of the Browning Hi-Power.

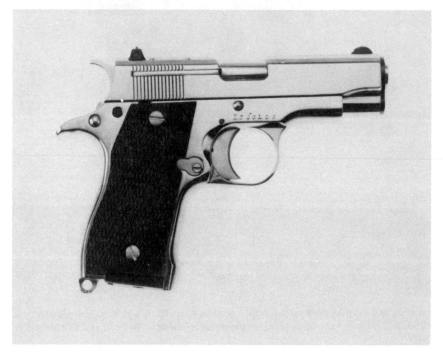

The Iver Johnson Pony is a Colt-style pistol similar to the 380 Government Model, only slightly more compact. The pistol is ideal for those who want a 1911-style pistol chambered in .380. Photo courtesy of Iver Johnson.

Specifications

Overall length: 6 inches
Weight (unloaded): 1.25 lbs.
Barrel length: 3.1 inches
Magazine capacity: 6

LLAMA IIIA

Unfortunately, the Llama pistols aren't noted either for innovative design or reliability. The Llama IIIA is modeled after the Browning pistols; it even has an outdated grip safety in addition to its thumb safety. The IIIA works only in single action and fires from a locked breech. The pistol has a ventilated rib of dubious use down its top.

Many Llama IIIAs have a highly polished surface in the blued models which make them less than ideal for combat use. The satin finished models are less reflective.

Takedown is similar to that of the 1911-A1 .45 auto.

Specifications

Overall length: 6.5 inches
Weight (unloaded): 1.44 lbs.
Barrel length: 3.69 inches

MANURHIN PP

This pistol is identical to the Walther and differs only in the "Walther" and "Made in Germany" markings. The reason for this is that the Walther pistols are made by Manurhin and assembled in Germany where they receive their German markings. See the Walther PP section for more information.

MKE

The MKE *(Makina ve Kimya Endustrisi Kurumu),* made in Turkey, is a Walther PP copy. The only difference is a slight variation in the finger rest of the floor plate and pistol-grip plates.

The Llama IIIA is modeled after the Browning pistols and even has a grip safety in addition to its thumb safety. The pistol works in the single-action mode and fires from a locked breech. This pistol might be ideal for those interested in a "baby" 1911-A1 chambered in .380 ACP. Photo courtesy of Stoeger Industries.

SEECAMP

The Seecamp pistol was originally chambered for .25 ACP but has been rechambered for .32 ACP. Not just any .32, however. The pistol is made to fire only the potent Winchester Silvertips. The slide and special recoil-delaying cut in the barrel's chamber are made to allow the pistol to function well with the Silvertips. Do not try any other type of ammunition; it may cause a malfunction or even damage the pistol with extended firing.

The Seecamp uses a double-action trigger coupled with a hammer that follows the slide forward so that every consecutive shot has to be fired double action. This eliminates the manual safety and makes the pistol relatively safe to carry with a round in the chamber.

The magazine release is located on the grip base, which is good on a gun the size of most hide-away .22s and .25s. One shortcoming may be the use of a magazine disconnector safety, though this design feature is not too great a consideration.

The Seecamp points well and functions fairly well. It is worthy of consideration as a .32 ACP pistol not much larger than many small .22 autos.

Field-stripping is simple if unorthodox. Remove the magazine and cycle the weapon to be sure the pistol is empty; empty the magazine and reinsert it; pull the slide back so that the disassembly hole in the slide lines up with the slide latch; depress the slide latch with a nail or small punch inserted through the hole in the slide; and lift and remove the slide. Reassembly is a reversal of this procedure.

Specifications

Overall length: 4.25 inches
Weight (unloaded): 0.75 lbs.
Barrel length: 2 inches
Magazine capacity: 6

SIG-SAUER P-230

The P-230 is designed around the SIG-Sauer P-220, but operates by blowback with a fixed barrel. It was introduced in 1977 and makes an ideal companion pistol for the P-220.

The pistol is available in both .32 and .380; .22 LR and the unusual 9x18mm (Police) used by some German police units are also seen. The pistol has an internal safety coupled to its double-action trigger. Its design completely dispenses with a manual safety; a hammer drop lever is located above its left grip panel. Unfortunately, the P-230 has the awkward base-of-the-grip magazine release that European designers seem to like.

A disassembly latch is located on the left side of the frame just above the front of the trigger guard; disassembly is similar to that of the 9mm Luger SIG-Sauer pistols.

Specifications

Overall length: 6.5 inches
Weight (unloaded): 1 lb.
Barrel length: 3.75 inches
Magazine capacity: 7 rounds in .380;
8 rounds, .32

STAR

In the 1920s Star Bonifacio Echeverria, S.A., of Eibar, created a number of pistols based on the Colt/Browning designs, many of them chambered in .32 and .380 ACP and operating in a straight blowback mode.

Star pistols chambered for .32 and .380 ACP have little to offer which isn't found on other pistols except, perhaps, to someone wanting a pistol whose controls resemble those on larger-caliber Colt/Browning weapons.

TARGA/EXCAM GT32/GT380

Targa pistols are manufactured in Italy and imported by Excam. They come in either a blue or chrome finish as well as engraved models; nylon and wood grips are available. The XE models have a double-row magazine, while the standard models have a single-row magazine. The finish, trigger pull, and design are not outstanding, but the guns function fairly well and their prices are low.

Specifications

Overall length: 7.38 inches
Weight (unloaded): 1.63 lbs. (1.75, XE models)
Barrel length: 4.86 inches
Magazine capacity: 6 (12 rounds XE)

Many inexpensive Italian pistols are imported into the United States. The finish, trigger pull and design of the pistols are not outstanding, but the guns often function fairly well and their low prices allow a little gunsmith work to be done on them if needed to tune them up for very reliable functioning.

TITAN PISTOLS

These cheap blowback pistols are made in Italy and sometimes assembled in the United States to get around the GCA. They are chambered for low-powered rounds like .22 LR, .32 ACP, and .380 ACP. They have some good design features but are often not well finished or dependable. It is probably best to spend more money on a different pistol.

VZ 50 AND 50/70

These pistols are little more than copies of the Walther PP. The only changes are the use of a disassembly catch at the front of the trigger guard, a spring clip that allows the grip panels to be readily removed, a frame-mounted thumb safety, and a rather poorly designed magazine release on the grip base. This pistol is a poorly executed Walther rip-off.

WALTHER PP, PPK, AND VARIATIONS

While the Walther PP was not the first double-action automatic, it was the first successful double-action automatic. And it has been successful for a long time.

The weapon was designed by Fritz Walther, the son of Carl Walther who founded the Walther Company in 1886. The PP was introduced in 1929 and became the standard weapon for many European law-enforcement agencies. "PP" stands for *Polizei Pistole* (Police Pistol). The PPK, a version with a shorter barrel and grip and a magazine that holds one less cartridge, was introduced a few months

The Walther PP series of weapons has enjoyed great popularity since its introduction. The weapons have been used by everyone, from British spies to the German Gestapo; the Walther PP enjoys as much notoriety in real life as in fiction. Because of the subsonic speed of most bullets fired from the Walther, these weapons also lend themselves well to use with a silencer, as shown here. Photo courtesy of Jonathon Arthur Ciener.

after the PP. The PPK *(Polizei Pistole Kriminal)* took its name from the German detective division, the *Kriminalamt.*

PP weapons have enjoyed great popularity from the beginning, with the PPK being one of the favorite weapons of German soldiers and the Gestapo. Following World War II, the United States gave the Walther plant to the Soviets; Fritz Walther escaped ahead of the new owners with only a few hours to spare and with a suitcase full of blueprints. He successfully defended his patent rights and licensed the Manurhin company in France to build his pistols. Even after Germany was permitted to resume production of firearms, German Walthers were actually made in the Manurhin plant with only a few assembly operations, bluing, and marking occurring in Germany.

In 1968 the United States Congress passed the Gun Control Act which banned the importation of the smaller PPK. (PPKs already in the States could be sold freely.) This ban led to the PPK/S *(Polizei Pistole Kriminal/Special),* which was simply a PPK slide, barrel, and recoil spring mounted on a PP frame, which made the weapon big enough to conform to the U.S. law. Walther started manufacturing this version of the pistol in 1969. Interestingly, many shooters who have fired all three versions of the PP prefer the PPK/S.

In 1978, work was started under the direction of Interarms at the Ranger Manufacturing Plant in Gadsen, Alabama, on a licensed copy of the .380 ACP PPK/S. Late in 1985, Interarms/Ranger Manufacturing started tooling up for the production of

the regular PPK and its sister pistol, the .22 LR TPH. So, although these two pistols are "too dangerous" to import, they will now be readily available in their made-in-U.S.A. form.

All Walther PP variants operate by straight blowback and are most commonly chambered for .380 ACP, though .32 ACP, .25 ACP (manufactured before World War II), and .22 LR versions are sometimes found (these .22 versions should not be confused with the Walther TPH which is a different pistol, though very similar to the PP guns). Steel and aluminum frames, long slide versions, long grip models, and even an experimental selective-fire version have all been made at one time or another.

The Walther's barrel is permanently mounted to the frame and serves as the guide rod for the recoil spring. The thumb safety is mounted on the slide and locks the firing pin and blocks it from the hammer, as well as dropping the hammer when engaged. A frame-mounted internal safety also blocks the firing pin unless the trigger is pulled back; this allows the pistol to be carried with the slide safety in the fire position and a round in the chamber. Coupled with the double-action trigger, this makes the PP an ideal pocket pistol which can be brought to fire by simply squeezing the trigger. Unfortunately, the magazine release is in a rather awkward position.

Most PP/PPKs have a loaded chamber indicator in the form of a rod which protrudes from the rear of the slide; if dirty, this sometimes doesn't retract on an empty chamber. It's a good idea to pull back the slide slightly to check for a chambered round rather than relying on the indicator rod. The slide locks open after the last round. This allows a quick reload. Since there is no slide release, an empty magazine must be removed before the slide can be closed.

The PP/PPK continues to be well liked and used, especially as a backup gun, by police and citizens worldwide. A huge number of copies and variations are currently made. The most notable are the Astra Constable, the Czechoslovakian Vz50 and Vz50/70, the Hungarian Walam, the Italian Bernardelli Model 60, the Turkish MKE, and the Charter Arms 79K/40 pistols. The Soviets were impressed with the PP/PPK as well: they developed a nearly uncontrollable selective-fire version, the Stechkin, and the *Pistolet Makarova* (PM) chambered for a large 9x18 mm Soviet pistol round. These and other versions are now made by other companies and countries, since the patent rights to the pistol's design have expired (and would be ignored by most communist countries, anyway).

PP/PPK pistols are excellent combat choices if you must use something less potent than the 9mm Luger. The pistols are noted for their reliability and ease of use.

Field-stripping is quite simple for the various PPs. Remove the magazine and cycle the weapon to be sure it's empty; pull down on the trigger guard to release the slide block; pull the slide back and lift the rear of it clear of the frame; and push the slide forward off the barrel. Reassembly is basically the reverse of this procedure.

Specifications for the PP

Overall length: 6.8 inches
Weight (unloaded): 1.5 lbs.
Barrel length: 3.9 inches
Magazine capacity: 8

9mm and .38 Super

Unfortunately, the Thompson/LaGarde tests conducted for the U.S. military in 1904 put small-caliber bullets into a poor light. These tests were flawed by modern standards in that they used too few test subjects (only sixteen steers and cows and two horses) as well as inappropriate test media (ten cadavers—live tissue behaves very differently from dead). The experimenters also assumed that large-caliber bullets were superior to 9mm/.38 regardless of velocity, especially since the U.S. had had poor experiences in combat with a slow-moving .38 round.

What the tests actually proved was that expanding bullets are probably necessary for combat. Here's what Louis La Garde wrote about his tests:

> "None of the full-jacketed [bullets] . . . showed the necessary shock effect or stopping power for a service weapon. . . . it was recommended that . . . the point of the jacket should be made very thin and that the lead core be made of softer lead than that of any of the bullets tested. The object of this was to invite mushrooming."

But of course that was against the conventions of war and couldn't be done. The U.S. adopted the .45 caliber pistol, which everyone thought was the correct caliber even before the tests were conducted.

Most modern authorities now agree that an expanding bullet is superior regardless of caliber; many feel the 9mm Luger is superior to the .45 ACP even when both use expanding bullets. The 9mm Luger can be an excellent defensive round and strikes a nice compromise between penetration and so-called "stopping power." Over-penetration is a consideration since police and citizens who use a pistol for self-defense must often do so in areas where a penetrating round would be dangerous to innocent bystanders. With an FMJ bullet, the 9mm Luger is as poor as many others, though recent tests suggest it might still be better than the .45 ACP. If you must use non-expanding bullets, CCI's 115-grain Blazer bullets tend to tumble upon impact and create nearly as large a wound channel as many expanding bullets.

Another consideration when choosing a defensive pistol for use with blunt-tipped expanding bullets is that the gun must chamber and function reliably with various hollow-point bullet nose configurations. Regardless of the nose configuration, the 9mm Luger 115-grain bullet seems to give the best functioning in most automatic actions—although this can vary from pistol to pistol.

Because of the 9mm Luger's small size, most modern combat automatics have large-capacity magazines, giving extra firepower when needed. However, many people feel pistol magazines holding 7 to 8 rounds are perfectly adequate and prefer the thinner grips possible with the single-column magazine. Also, pistols holding fewer than ten rounds often are more easily concealed.

A number of companies offer 9mm Luger and/or .38 Super versions of their .45 ACP pistols. Among these are Arminex Trifire, Auto Ordnance, Caspian Arms, Colt, O.D.I. Viking, Randall, Springfield Armory, and Star. For more information on these pistols, see the .45 ACP chapter.

ASP

The ASP was a custom pistol created during the early 1960s by chopping a S&W Model 39. The work was done by Chic Gaylord and Paris Theodore and—with a lot of ad hype about "spy and secret courier" use—the shooting public bought the pistols at premium prices. The ASP was well thought out, however, and provided a pistol the size of a .380 automatic which fired the much more potent 9mm Luger cartridge.

The ASP pistols had transparent Lexan stocks which allowed the shooter to see how many rounds were left in the magazine. The barrel was throated and the feed ramp smoothed to function well with hollow-point ammunition. Additionally, the magazine disconnect safety was removed.

Unfortunately, the pistols used a "guttersnipe" sight, which gets misaligned easily and is hard to use accurately at long range. While the lack of a good sight is not much of a disadvantage in a hide-away gun designed for close range combat, it is still less than ideal.

The ASP was a good idea and certainly filled an important niche. It also spurred a number of companies like Detonics and even Smith & Wesson to create similar pistols. But the ASP is not nearly as safe or reliable as more modern combat pistols, and is better left to the collector.

ASTRA A-80

Many people considered Spanish pistols to be shoddy following the flooding of the U.S. market with cheap Spanish weapons in the early 1930s. To some extent this may be true, though the quality of Astra, Llama, and Star pistols are currently as good as many others.

Astra automatic pistols date back to a version of the Mauser 1896, the 900 and 902, and some less-than-ideal pistols like the 1921, 400, and 600. Since then, Astra has created some worthwhile combat pistols, the best of which is probably the A-80 currently offered in 9mm Luger, .38 Super, and .45 ACP.

The A-80 uses a hammer-lowering safety and a double-action trigger. Thanks to an internal trigger-coupled safety, the pistol can be safely carried with a round in the chamber and quickly fired double-action.

The pistol uses a steel frame and is available in blued or chrome finish. Left-handed models are available with the hammer-drop lever on the right side of the frame.

Overall, the A-80 is a good pistol, but unfortunately its magazine release is at the base of the pistol grip, making it less than ideal for combat.

To field-strip, remove the magazine and cycle the weapon to be sure it's empty; turn the disassembly lever on the right side of the frame down; push the slide forward off the frame; carefully push the recoil spring and rod toward the front of the slide to release and lift the spring and rod out; and remove the barrel from the slide. Reassembly is the reverse of this procedure.

Specifications

Overall length: 7.5 inches
Weight (unloaded): 2.17 lbs.
Barrel length: 3.94 inches
Magazine capacity: 15 rounds
(9 rounds, .45 ACP)

BENELLI B76

This is a well-made pistol with a serious design flaw: it feeds reliably only with full-metal jacket bullets. This problem is coupled to the angle of the pistol grip and can't be cured with polishing of the feed ramp, etc. Along with the 8-round magazine, this makes the B76 a less-than-ideal combat weapon.

BERETTA 1951/1952

In 1950, the Italian Army adopted the 9mm Luger round for their pistols. Tullio Marengoni, who designed Italian military sidearms used through World War II, went back to the drawing board to produce the Model 1951 (also known as the Model 951) in 9mm Luger as well as a sister pistol, the 1952, chambered in 7.62mm Luger. Unlike other Beretta pistols, this weapon fired from a locked breech system borrowed from the German P-38.

The pistol uses an improved 1934-style sear but adds a takedown lever on the right side of the frame. Unfortunately, the crossbolt safety located at the top of the grip panel is far from ideal. While quick to release, it practically requires two hands to engage. The magazine release is little better and is located in the lower left area of the pistol grip. Like the 1934 pistols, the 1951's magazine has a little finger hook; many shooters find this projection unnecessary due to the length of the grip.

All in all, the 1951 has rather poor human engineering but is also very reliable. Because of this reliability, it has been adopted by the Italian, Israeli, and Egyptian armies.

In an effort to improve the pistol's handling characteristics, in 1969 a much welcomed slide-mounted thumb safety lever was adopted. A selective-fire model, the 1951A (also known as the 1951R), was also made, with an extended magazine, beefed up parts, weighted slide, rate-of-fire retarding device, and forward grip assembly to help control the pistol in automatic fire. Apparently the selective-fire model was never sold in great numbers.

Field-stripping is quite simple. Remove the magazine and cycle the action to be sure the pistol is empty; pull the slide back until the disassembly latch lines up with the notch in the slide; push the disassembly latch forward toward the muzzle; pull the slide up and off the frame; carefully push the recoil spring and rod toward the front of the slide to release and lift the spring and rod out; and remove the barrel. Reassembly is a reversal of this procedure.

Specifications

Overall length: 8 inches
Weight (unloaded): 1.9 lbs.
Barrel length: 4.5 inches
Barrel twist: 6 grooves, right-hand
Magazine capacity: 8

BERETTA 92 SERIES

The 92 series was introduced in 1976. A number of variations have since been created with differences in the slide release, magazine release, and safety placement; magazine capacity; and shortening of the overall height and length.

The 92 series pistols have very thin grips compared to other double-column 9mm pistols. This is due to thin grip panels and an external trigger lever (early critics of the trigger design felt that this might cause accidental firing or jams but both possibilities proved unfounded in tests). The magazine

The Beretta 92 pistols have developed a reputation for extremely reliable functioning with a wide range of ammunition, and many feel that the Beretta 92-F (shown here) is the best and most reliable pistol now available. Some version of the Beretta pistol is now the official side arm for a number of countries' armies, as well as for a number of police units in both the United States and Europe.

also seats quite high. This allows a very short feed ramp, which in turn means that the 92 series will easily chamber a wide range of bullet configurations with little problem. The Beretta trademark—the cut-out section of the barrel—has also paid off in preventing extraction problems. These last two points have surprised and pleased gun writers and test personnel: it isn't rare for a Beretta pistol to suffer zero failures to feed and extract when tested!

The various models of the 92 series are distinguished in the following ways: Model 92 has a frame-mounted thumb safety (non-ambidextrous) and a magazine release at the lower-left side of the pistol grip; Model 92S, introduced in 1978, has a slide-mounted safety which also serves as a hammer drop/firing-pin block. In 1979 the 92S-1 was created for testing by the U.S. armed forces (as the XM9) with a slide-mounted, ambidextrous safety, grooved front and back strap on the pistol grip, and a reversible magazine release on the side of the pistol grip behind the trigger; the 92SB was the commercial version of the 92S-1 and was marketed in 1981. Also unveiled in 1981 was the 92SB-C, the compact version of the 92SB with a 13-round magazine.

The 92F (also known as the 92SB-F) was the modified version of the 92SB which was finally adopted by the U.S. military and is currently being sold to a number of U.S. police units and on the commercial market. This model is similar to the 92SB but has a cut-out area in the pistol grip plate for easier release of the thumb safety, an enlarged and squared-off trigger guard, matte black finish applied over the metal, slightly different grip contours with a flare at the grip base, a thicker magazine plate, a chromed barrel, a lanyard mount rotated 90 degrees from that of the SB, and taller sights with white glow-in-the-dark inserts. It should be noted that the inserts shine brightly *after* being exposed to a bright light. However, if the pistol is kept in a covered holster or drawer, the sights may not glow in the dark. Therefore, anyone needing this capability must be sure the pistol is exposed to light before it is taken into the dark.

Two versions of the 92F are offered, the standard pistol and the 92F-C, which is the 13-round chopped version of the automatic. Buyers have the choice between plastic and wooden grips, designated with a "P" or "W" in the model number. A variation of the 92 series is also made by Taurus Firearms, which purchased the Brazilian Beretta

plant. For more information on these pistols, see the Taurus section.

All Beretta 92s have a loaded chamber indicator consisting of a red section of the extractor which is exposed when a round is chambered. The SB and SB-F models all have a reversible magazine-release button so that a left-handed shooter can easily turn the button around. Coupled with the ambidextrous manual safety, these weapons finally take the left-handed shooter into account.

Perhaps the biggest coup in Beretta's marketing of the 92 series came when a modified 92SB (the 92SB-F) became the new M9 pistol of the U.S. armed forces in January 1985. Thus, the Beretta 92F will probably enjoy the same wealth of accessories and military-surplus spare parts that the Colt 1911 pistol has. Many shooters realize this and a number of buyers are already jumping onto the Beretta bandwagon.

It is also probable that a lot of training aids will become available with the police/military use of the pistol. Several such aids are already on the market, sold by Daisy Air Rifles. One is their Model 09 "soft air" gun which fires small plastic pellets; this is ideal for training new shooters to handle the Beretta pistol safely and has a limited use for safely practicing quick draws and instinctive shooting in areas where a real firearm can't be safely used. For inexpensive, quiet indoor practice, the Daisy Model 92 Powerline BB pistol is ideal, since it allows semiauto firing for realistic practice engagements of multiple targets. Both air guns have been carefully designed to duplicate the size and shape of the Beretta pistols and should be considered as purchases for Beretta 92 owners.

All versions of the Beretta 92 pistols can fire their first shot double-action and can be safely carried with the thumb safety in the fire position and the hammer down, thanks to a firing-pin block which isn't released until the trigger is pulled all the way back. It is also possible to carry the Model 92 (but not the SB models) cocked and locked with the safety on and the hammer back for single-action firing of the first round. Models with the frame-mounted safety/hammer drop lever can also be modifed for cock and lock carry by a gunsmith. (While this makes the weapon fire single action for its first shot, the thumb safety is somewhat awkward to release and any speed gained by the modification may be lost. Possibly an aftermarket extended safety will alleviate this problem. With the SB models, the best speed and safety probably result when the Beretta pistols are left unmodified with the slide safety left in "fire" position and the first shot fired double-action.) Since the trigger guard is large enough to allow firing while wearing gloves, not having to fool with a manual safety would also be ideal in cold weather.

A wide variety of holsters is available for the Beretta 92 pistols. The ambidextrous U.S. military UM84 is currently available from Brigade Quartermasters in either black, olive drab, or camouflage for $40. Alessi and Milt Sparks have several excellent concealable leather holsters designed for the 92. At the low end of the budget scale—but still of high quality—are the Uncle Mike's holsters, available at most gun stores.

In addition to the owner's manual that comes with the 92F pistol, many shooters should also try to obtain the U.S. Army manual, which contains information not found in the factory manual. This manual is available from Sierra Supply.

The Beretta 92 pistols have developed a reputation for extremely reliable functioning with a wide range of ammunition. Many people feel the 92F is the best and most reliable pistol now available. Some version of the Beretta 92 pistol is now the official sidearm for a number of armies and police units in the United States and Europe. The Beretta 92 pistols are well designed, and it is probable that the pistol will remain popular well into the twenty-first century.

Field-stripping is quite simple. Remove the magazine and cycle the weapon to be sure the chamber is empty; push in the disassembly release button on the left side and rotate the disassembly lever on the right side of the frame downward; push the slide forward off the frame; carefully push the recoil spring and rod toward the front of the slide to release and lift the spring and rod out; and depress the locking block plunger (just below the chamber) and lift out the barrel. Reassembly is the reverse of this procedure; be sure the barrel plunger is again depressed when reassembling the pistol.

Specifications

Overall length: 8.5 inches
(7.8 compact models)
Weight (unloaded): 2.2 lbs. (2.1, compact)
Barrel length: 4.9 inches (4.3 compact)
Barrel twist: 6 grooves, right-hand
Magazine capacity: 13, 15, or 20 rounds

BERETTA 92 SB TYPE M

The 92SB Type M is similar to the 92 series pistols. Its main difference is a single-column magazine. It has the small overall size of the 92 compacts and, like the other compact Berettas, lacks a lanyard ring. It also lacks the reversible magazine-release button. Slide safety, magazine release, etc., are all identical to the 92 series.

The Beretta 98 and 99 models are nearly identical to the Type M but are chambered for 7.65 Luger. Disassembly is basically the same as 92 series pistols.

Specifications

Overall length: 7.8 inches
Weight (unloaded): 2 lbs.
Barrel length: 4.3 inches
Barrel twist: 6 grooves, right-hand
Magazine capacity: 8

BERETTA 93R

This pistol appears to be a variation of the 92 series. It has a three-round burst mode in addition to semiauto fire. The barrel length is 6.14 inches, which Beretta testing indicated was the longest length that could be easily drawn from a concealed holster. This maximum length increases the velocity of the 9mm bullets and helps stabilize the pistol during firing. In order to make the weapon more controllable in burst fire, the barrel has compensator cuts which also cut down on muzzle flash. A forward grip flips down from under the front of the frame and is coupled with an oversized trigger guard designed to accept the thumb of the off hand for greater control. A detachable stock folds up to be carried concealed in a pouch.

The selector is mounted where one might expect to find a frame-mounted thumb safety (three dots for burst fire and one dot for semiauto fire). The safety is just behind the selector; the up position (red dot exposed) is fire while the down position is safe. While the weapon will accept the standard Model 92 15-round magazine, it would normally use a 20-round magazine. The pistol fires in single-action only to simplify the mechanisms and can be carried cocked and locked with the safety engaged.

The magazine release of early 93Rs was located at the bottom of the grip, but has been moved to a much more convenient position just behind the trigger guard.

The 93R has seen only limited work with body-guards and possibly anti-terrorist squads; the market for such a weapon must be extremely small at best. However, the three-round burst feature and concealable detachable stock may make the idea of the machine pistol finally come to life.

Field-stripping is nearly identical to the 92 series weapons.

Specifications

Overall length: 9.5 inches (23.6 with stock)
Weight (unloaded): 2.5 lbs. (3 lbs. with stock)
Barrel length: 6.1 inches
Barrel twist: 6 grooves, right-hand
Magazine capacity: 20

BERNARDELLI P018

The P018 is made by Armes de Chasse of Italy which has just started exporting the pistol to the United States. The double-action, all-steel pistol is available in a variety of finishes as well as in a chopped version holding 14 rounds rather than the standard 16. The P018 pistol also has a .380 ACP counterpart that is nearly identical except for chambering.

At the time of this writing, the P018 was un-available for testing but it seems to offer great promise. Apparently some are being marketed with magazine releases placed on the left side of the grip just behind the trigger guard while others have the release at the grip base. The pistol also has a thumb safety located on the slide just above the pistol grip which locks the hammer, slide, and trigger, as well as an auto-locking internal safety.

The Bernardelli P018 pistols are being imported into the United States by Springfield Armory. These double-action, all-steel pistols are available in a chopped version that holds 14 rounds as well as the standard 16-round version. The P018 pistols also have a .380 ACP counterpart that is nearly identical to the 9mm Luger pistols, except for chambering. Photo courtesy of Springfield Armory.

BROWNING P-35 HI-POWER

The Browning Hi-Power is among the best 9mm automatics available. Many consider it *the* best single-action automatic. The weapon was introduced for sale in 1935 as the P-35 by Fabrique Nationale in Liège, Belgium. Company publicity gave it the name "Hi-Power" (variations of this include "High-Power," "HP," "Grand Puissance," and "GP"). Whether the "Hi-Power" moniker was tacked on because the pistol was chambered for the 9mm Luger or because of its large magazine capacity is unclear.

Early prototypes were produced for the French Army. These had 15-round magazines to meet French military specifications. When the French decided against the pistol, Browning shortened the grip to make it more comfortable and reduced the magazine capacity to 13 rounds.

The Hi-Power was John Browning's last firearm design and was first produced in 1923 with the patents being awarded to him in 1927, just a few months after his death. It is interesting to note how far ahead of its time the Hi-Power was with its 9mm Luger chambering, lack of a grip safety and barrel bushing, and high-capacity magazine.

An examination of the Hi-Power prototype and patent drawings show some innovations not incorporated on the final model. The original lacks a manual thumb safety and hold-open lever and uses a striker rather than a hammer, a single-column magazine, and a fold-down trigger as a safety. The prototype also had much thinner lines, with more metal milled from the slide and frame. Whether Browning would have approved of the changes between the final production pistol and the prototype remains open to debate; apparently many changes in the design were created by Dieudonne J. Saive, a "pupil" of Browning's.

The Hi-Power was originally slated for public release in 1929 but was delayed until 1934 because of the American stock market crash. The Hi-Power was adopted by the Belgian Army shortly after the pistol was introduced, with a 10-round magazine and shortened slide. It was also adopted by the Belgian Congo, China, Denmark, El Salvador,

The Browning Hi-Power is among the best 9mm automatics available. Many consider it the best single-action automatic. The weapon was introduced for sale in 1935 and designated the P-35 by Fabrique Nationale in Liège, Belgium. Company publicity gave it the name "High Power." Photo courtesy of Browning.

Ethiopia, Holland, Indonesia, Lithuania, Paraguay, Siam, Syria, and Venezuela. All these pistols vary only in magazine capacity, sight types, lanyard rings, and other slight modifications.

Following the German occupation of Belgium in 1940, the Hi-Power became a substitute German service sidearm; nearly 200,000 were made during this period. (Like other weapons made during the Nazi occupation, some of these weapons were sabotaged and are dangerous to shoot.) A number of FN engineers fled ahead of the Nazi forces and ended up in Canada, where they started making the Hi-Power at the John Inglis plant in Toronto. These weapons went to Nationalist China and later to Greece, Australia, Canada, and Britain.

Following World War II, the P-35 became the most widely used military handgun in the world. Production at the Inglis plant was discontinued and manufacture was carried on solely by FN. These new models are sometimes called the "Model 1946," with the adjustable sight version called the "Capitan" and the standard sight pistol marketed as the "Vigilante." Generally, both versions are known simply as "Hi-Powers" in the United States, where they are marketed by Browning.

In an effort to reverse declining sales in recent years, FN has marketed the double-action Hi-Power, featuring a double-action trigger and other minor improvements such as a heavier extractor, firing-pin safety coupled to the trigger, and a 15-round magazine. An ambidextrous hammer drop lever sits in the position occupied by the old safety; the hammer is bobbed, though serrations on its top permit thumb cocking. Whether this version will capture a share of the market remains to be seen.

Hi-Power variants are available on the surplus market, including ones with stock slots and tangent sights. Special extended magazines were also made by FN on special order to increase the firepower of these stocked pistols. For a time, a selective-fire version of the Hi-Power was sold by FN but these are currently quite rare. Some military surplus Hi-Powers have an adjustable tangent sight which is graduated to optimistic 500 and even 1,000 meter settings.

The operating principles of the Hi-Power are nearly identical to the Colt 1911. Both pistols have the same basic control layout. Parts are not, however, interchangeable, and many internal parts are much different. The Hi-Power, for example, uses a fixed cam in the barrel rather than a moving link; this newer arrangement gives better wear and more positive lockup.

The Hi-Power can be modified in several ways for combat. The thumb safety is rather small and awkward and can stand enlargement for easier engagement; most gunsmiths can order an enlarged safety to replace the standard one. Austin and Frank Behlert and Jim Hoag both offer these larger safeties.

Another useful modification is to remove the magazine safety. This allows you to shoot the weapon without a magazine in place, and will greatly improve the trigger pull, allowing empty magazines to drop freely from the pistol. The removal of the safety is easily carried out; its two parts are called the "plunger" and "plunger spring" in the owner's manual. It's a good idea also to have the cross pin that connects the magazine disconnector to the trigger removed so that it doesn't come loose and gum up the trigger. While you're having this work done, it would also be wise to have the gunsmith polish and deburr the trigger and sear as well as their levers for a better trigger pull. Because both the spur style and the rounded, hole-in-the-center style hammers are available for the Hi-Power, some users may wish to exchange hammers. The long spur is convenient for thumb cocking but tends to get snagged in bulky clothing and isn't as comfortable for concealed wear.

Extended magazine release levers are available from Pachmayr. These aid in quick reloading but care must be taken not to snag these when firing so that the slide is inadvertently locked open. (Since most gunfights are short, chances of accidentally locking the slide open with disastrous results are probably greater than losing the battle because of slowness in reloading with the extended magazine capacity of the Hi-Power.)

Some shooters find the Hi-Power's sights leave something to be desired. Two alternate sights found on many Hi-Powers are the S&W revolver sight (which requires some milling to get it into place—a major gunsmithing chore) and the Millett Custom Combat sight (which—unfortunately—also requires milling).

Finally, many shooters find the floor plates on the Hi-Power magazines too thin. This can mean a magazine doesn't get shoved fully into the magazine well. The easiest solution to this problem is to purchase some Pachmayr bumper pads. These rubber pads slip right onto the magazine and will cushion the base if you drop it.

Not all Browning Hi-Powers are created equal, as this expensive Louis XVI offered in the United States by Browning shows. In the past, a great number of variants of this pistol have been made, including Hi-Powers with stock slots and tangent sights as well as a selective-fire version of the pistol. Photo courtesy of Browning.

The large numbers of Hi-Powers available on the used and surplus market can be good buys. However, the lack of an automatic safety for the inertial firing pin and the need to take the manual safety off to cycle the slide make older Hi-Powers less safe than many newer pistols. At least from a safety standpoint, the single-action Hi-Power may be less than ideal.

Takedown is relatively simple. Remove the magazine and pull the slide back to be sure the weapon is unloaded; lock the slide open with the thumb safety; push out the slide release lever from right to left of the receiver; release the slide and allow it to run forward off the frame; carefully push the recoil spring and rod toward the front of the slide to release and lift the spring and rod out; and remove the barrel. Reassembly is the reverse of this procedure.

Specifications for Hi-Power (single action)

Overall length: 8 inches
Weight (unloaded): 2 lbs.
Barrel length: 4.75 inches
Barrel twist: right-hand, 6 grooves
Magazine capacity: 13 (14 with new magazines)

Specifications for Hi-Power (double action)

Overall length: 7.75 inches
Weight (unloaded): 2 lbs.
Barrel length: 4.75 inches
Barrel twist: right-hand, 6 grooves
Magazine capacity: 14

COLT "SSP"

During the last round of tests by the U.S. JSSAP (Joint Services Small Arms Program) to select a new military 9mm pistol, Colt Firearms dusted off a double-action 9mm pistol that had been in the prototype stage for at least ten years and entered it in the tests.

The pistol is designated the "SSP" (Stainless Steel Pistol) and differs markedly from Colt's 1911-A1. The SSP has a double-column magazine, ambidextrous slide mounted safety, and double-action trigger. The Colt look is in the control layout, shape of the slide, grip angle, rear sight, and Commander-style hammer. The SSP was introduced for the JSSAP tests with a dark gray matte finish. If this pistol is introduced on a commercial basis, it will probably have a more conventional finish since its frame, slide, and many parts are stainless steel.

The magazine release is located at the left rear of the trigger guard. The slide release extends back to the top of the left grip plate and a takedown lever is placed at the base of the slide release. A retractable lanyard is located at the grip base. The hammer-drop safety is similar to that of many other new automatics and the SSP has an internal firing-pin block which allows safe carrying with a round in the chamber.

Takedown is simple. Remove the magazine and pull the slide back to be sure the weapon is unloaded; keep the slide pulled to the rear and rotate the disassembly lever down and forward; push the safety into the fire position and push the slide forward off the frame; carefully push the recoil spring and rod toward the front of the slide to release and lift the spring and rod out; and remove the barrel. The hammer assembly can also be removed by removing the housing screw on the underside of the grip. Reassembly is the reverse of this procedure.

Specifications

Overall length: 8 inches
Weight (unloaded): 2.25 lbs.
Barrel length: 4.25 inches
Magazine capacity: 14

CZ 75

The CZ 75 is basically a double-action version of the Browning Hi-Power introduced in 1975. A military version has a ring hammer rather than a spur. The pistols are made in Strakoniče, Czechoslovakia.

Early models have short frame rails, no half-cock notch on the hammer, and a burr hammer. These pistols are not quite as reliable as the newer models, which are more desirable for combat use. Earlier pistols had a blue finish; current models have a black epoxy finish.

The CZ 75 has a machined steel frame, lacks

a magazine safety, and also has the safety mounted on the frame rather than the slide. Best of all, perhaps, is the double-stirrup trigger, which gives a smooth trigger pull. Unfortunately, the CZ 75 doesn't have an internal firing-pin safety; carrying the pistol with the hammer down is therefore a bit risky despite an inertial firing pin. However, the pistol can be carried cocked and locked, and the thumb safety is easily reached; this makes the CZ 75 as safe as the single-action Hi-Power or the 1911-A1 but less safe than pistols with integral trigger-coupled firing-pin safeties. This shortcoming and the fact that the pistol is hard to obtain in the United States makes it a better bet either to stick with a Browning or go with a modern double-action pistol.

Takedown is identical to the TZ-75/TA-90 Italian copies of the CZ 75.

Specifications

Overall length: 8 inches
Weight (unloaded): 2.2 lbs.
Barrel length: 4.72 inches
Magazine capacity: 15

DETONICS POCKET 9

When Smith & Wesson introduced its Model 39 double-action automatic, it wasn't long before the pistol was being chopped to a concealable size. Unlike most other hide-away guns, it fired the potent 9mm Luger.

Detonics sought to capture some of the S&W market with a pistol similar to the S&W 39 but made of stainless steel. Included in Detonics' design are a slide-mounted ambidextrous thumb safety/firing-pin block, magazine release at the rear of the hooked trigger guard, bobbed hammer, and double-action trigger. The sights are grooved into the top of the slide on all but the "380" model to keep them snag-free.

The standard model is the Pocket 9, with the Pocket 9LS having an extra long slide for added velocity. A highly polished Power 9 model (not ideal for combat purposes) and a similar pistol in .380 ACP, the Pocket 380, are also available.

The Detonics pistols make ideal hide-away or backup guns, though their recoil is severe. Unfortunately, the thumb safety works opposite to most others; fire position is down while safe is up.

Lack of an internal trigger-coupled safety makes carrying the pistol with a round in the chamber and the safety off less safe than one might hope. The hammer is rather hard to manipulate, but this is not normally a consideration with a double-action first shot capability. Sales of the Pocket 9 were clobbered by the introduction of the S&W 469. It will remain to be seen if the market can support both of these fine hide-aways.

Specifications for Power 9/Pocket 9

Overall length: 5.75 inches
Weight (unloaded): 1.6 lbs.
Barrel length: 3 inches
Magazine capacity: 6

Specifications for Pocket 9LS

Overall length: 6.9 inches
Weight (unloaded): 1.75 lbs.
Barrel length: 4 inches
Magazine capacity: 6

GLOCK 17

The Glock 17 was created by a Vienna company previously known mainly for cutlery products. It was designed by Gaston Glock, the director and chairman of the board of the Glock Company. Glock approached the design of the pistol as a modern engineer with extensive knowledge of plastics and metallurgy rather than a familiarity with past pistol design (although it is interesting to note that the ever-popular Browning Hi-Power style barrel locking system was finally used for basic lockup of the pistol with the recoil spring placed under the barrel). Work on the Glock 17 started late in 1980 and the finished pistol was adopted by the Austrian army in 1983, chosen over the Steyr 9B.

The pistol makes extensive use of plastics; the frame is made of plastic with metal inserts for the receiver/slide interface and the slide is a plastic extrusion with a machined bolt inside. The pistol uses a striker to simplify design. The simplified mechanism also allows the pistol grip to have a

Adopted by the Austrian Army in 1983, the Glock 17 makes the most of current trends toward the use of plastics and modern industrial techniques. The frame itself is plastic (with metal inserts for the receiver/slide interface), as is the plastic extrusion slide (with a machined bolt placed inside it). The magazine is mostly plastic with steel lips and spring. The use of a striker does away with the need of a hammer. Photo courtesy of Glock, Inc.

large "bubble" in its rear; this can be modified to give various grip pitches.

In keeping with the trend toward more plastic parts, the Glock 17 uses a plastic magazine with steel lips and spring. (The light weight of the magazine is not without its problems since empty magazines may fail to drop out fully without aid from the shooter. This is especially true with a little dirt in the pistol.) A square release is located on the left of the pistol grip behind the trigger guard. The release is slightly unprotected, so care should be taken not to carry the pistol in a holster which might inadvertently release the magazine.

Many shooters have trouble getting used to the trigger pull. Since the striker is always in the same position once the gun is loaded, the first shot has the same pull as all subsequent shots. While this seems like a good thing, it has some bad trade-offs; the slide must be pulled back to make the striker hit the round a second time in the case of a misfire, and the pull is heavier than many single-action pulls, though certainly low compared to other double-action pulls. The trigger pull has a two-stage feel to it. The first part is lighter while the last eighth of an inch becomes heavier (5 pounds) just before releasing the striker and firing the pistol. Total trigger pull is limited to a little less than a half inch.

The safety is mounted on the trigger and it is released by the trigger pull. Some shooters may dislike this safety, but it is better left in place.

Because the grip/magazine well is one molded piece of plastic, no grip plates are necessary and the grip is a lot thinner than that of other large-capacity magazines. This gives it less of a baseball-bat feel to shooters with smaller hands. The pistol's light weight causes felt recoil to be a little greater, but because of the comfortable grip and low barrel placement, it isn't as noticeable as one might think.

The Glock is reliable and, because of the use of plastics and modern manufacturing techniques, less expensive than comparable pistols. Although the American anti-gun movement claimed that the pistol didn't show up on airline detection equipment, this is not the case. In addition to being readily seen with X-ray equipment, the pistol contains over a pound of steel parts and is far from the "plastic gun" mentioned by the press.

Specifications

Overall length: 7.25 inches

Weight (unloaded): 1.45 lbs.
Barrel length: 4.75 inches
Magazine capacity: 17

HECKLER & KOCH P7

Following the Palestinian terrorist attack during the 1972 Olympics, the West German police decided they needed a handgun which didn't require operating a safety before being fired. Heckler and Koch created the PSP to meet this requirement.

The PSP fulfilled specifications by placing a grip safety/cocking lever along the front strap of the pistol grip. Grasping the weapon tightly cocks a striker so the weapon can be fired via single-action. While it takes fifteen pounds of pressure to cock this lever, only a little over one pound will keep it in place. When the grip is relaxed or the weapon released, the front strap pops back out and the safety is back on.

The weapon operates by gas-retarded blowback, which allows a fixed barrel and a small overall size. The PSP is offered commercially as the P7 pistol.

During the 1980 tests conducted by the U.S. military for a new pistol, H&K submitted a version of the P7, which added an ambidextrous magazine release behind the trigger guard and increased the thickness of material under the gas tube so that the area by the trigger didn't overheat with extended firing, and increased the magazine capacity to 13 rounds. This unique multi-angled magazine makes the new version little thicker than the original 8-round model.

Although the pistol didn't capture the military contract, H&K marketed a commercial model designated the P7-M13 (or P7-A13). A new version of the P7 with the behind-the-trigger-guard magazine release is also available with an 8-round magazine and is designated the P7-M8. A .45 ACP model may also be marketed. The various models of the P-7 have been favorably received by many law enforcement groups in the States.

Another P7 variant soon to be marketed is the P7-K3 kit gun which can be adapted to .22 LR, .32 ACP, or .380 ACP by changing slides, barrels, and magazines. Yet another variant is the P7-PP8, an 8mm pistol designed to use a special plastic training cartridge. The P7-PP8 has a large blue dot on each side of the slide to show that it is only a training pistol.

The small, flat design of the P7 makes it ideal

The H&K P7-M13 (or P7-A13) holds 13 rounds and has a unique grip safety which cocks its striker for a single-action first shot. This version of the P7 has a behind-the-trigger-guard magazine release that is ambidextrous.

The H&K P7-M8 is nearly identical to the original PSP, but has a behind-the-trigger-guard magazine release that is ambidextrous. Because of its flat design and small dimensions, this pistol is often chosen as a hideaway weapon by those who want the power of the 9mm Luger.

as a hide-away gun. When choosing a holster for this pistol, be sure that the front strap isn't depressed and the pistol cocked when it is being carried. One of the best-designed holsters is the Alessi "Speed Holster," originally designed for Canadian anti-terrorist squads. The holster is made so that the pistol is released once the cocking lever is squeezed. (The holster is available from Alessi for $39.)

Field-stripping the P7 is quite simple. Remove the magazine and cycle the pistol to be sure it's empty; pull the slide back while pushing on the disassembly button at the left rear of the frame; and lift the rear of the slide up and allow it to run forward off the frame. Care should be taken to clean out the gas tube area carefully to assure trouble-free operation. Reassembly is the reverse of this procedure.

Specifications

Overall length: 6.54 inches
Weight (unloaded): 2.16 lbs.
Barrel length: 4.13 inches
Magazine capacity: 8 (13 rounds in P7-M13)

HECKLER & KOCH P9/P9S

The P9, and its double-action version, the P9S, uses a roller-locking system similar to that of the Heckler and Koch rifles. The pistol makes use of steel stampings to simplify manufacture. Its internal hammer has a small cocked indicator that protrudes from the rear of the frame.

Early P9s were made with a polygon barrel which gave the bullet its spin without cutting grooves in the barrel. While this has a number of advantages (at least in theory), current barrels seem to be made with the standard grooves and lands. Optional 5 and 5-1/2 inch barrel lengths are found on some P9s.

The pistol has a somewhat awkward cocking/decocking lever on the left side behind the trigger guard. This can, with a bit of effort, be used to raise the hammer for single-action fire on the first shot or, with the safety engaged, to lower the hammer with the trigger. Unfortunately, this lever requires that a magazine release be located at the base of the pistol grip, which—coupled with the 9-round magazine capacity and large size—makes the P9 a somewhat limited combat pistol. The P9S is also available in .45 ACP and 7.62mm Luger.

Field-stripping is as follows. Remove the magazine and cycle the pistol to be sure it's empty; depress the latch inside the front of the trigger guard and push the slide forward; lift the slide up and off the frame; and push the barrel forward in the slide and remove it from the lower side of the slide. The bolt head can also be removed, but this requires a bit more work: use one end of the barrel extension to depress the locking latch between the bolt head and the slide. During reassembly, be sure the large end of the recoil spring goes toward the front of the frame and that the assembly notches in the frame are lined up with the lugs in the slide. Once the slide is in place, pull it back to cock the hammer and release it.

Specifications

Overall length: 7.5 inches

Weight (unloaded): 1.9 lbs.
Barrel length: 4 inches
Magazine capacity: 9 (8—7.62mm; 7—.45 ACP)

HECKLER & KOCH VP-70M/VP-70Z

The VP-70M pistol was introduced in the early 1970s. It was designed to be used with a stock as a machine pistol with three-round bursts as well as semiautomatic fire. A selector mounted at the top of the stock also contains the cams to count the three-round burst. Unfortunately, the selector can't be reached by the firing hand thumb of right-handed shooters. When the stock is removed, the pistol fires semiauto only. The stock, which doubles as a holster, is less than steady when fastened to the pistol and tends to wobble a bit between the two joints; while this doesn't really harm accuracy, it can be disconcerting and may have hurt sales. Adding to the problems, the stock locks into place rather noisily.

A bracket/strap accessory is normally used to mount the stock/holster for belt carry. The latch which locks the pistol in the stock/holster is plastic and tends to wear out with time. It would be wise to replace it with a metal latch if the pistol will be carried in the stock for a long period of time.

In an effort to gain larger sales, Heckler and Koch also markets the pistol in a semiauto-only form as the VP-70Z. This pistol is nearly identical to the stocked version but doesn't have mounting cuts in the grip or the mounting bracket at the rear of the upper frame.

As a pistol, the VP-70 is quite different in that each shot requires a double-action pull. The trigger pull comes in two stages: the first is heavy, followed by a slight letup, then a lighter pull which releases the striker. Unfortunately, the double-action trigger pull of the VP-70 is generally quite heavy; this is an important consideration.

The simple double-action trigger and hammerless design greatly reduce the internal parts; disregarding springs and the magazine, there are only four moving parts in the VP-70. To further lower manufacturing costs, the pistol uses a plastic frame with the fixed barrel fastened to it. Because it is double action, the pistol is often encountered without a safety; when a safety is placed on the weapon, it goes at the rear of the trigger guard.

The magazine release is awkwardly placed at

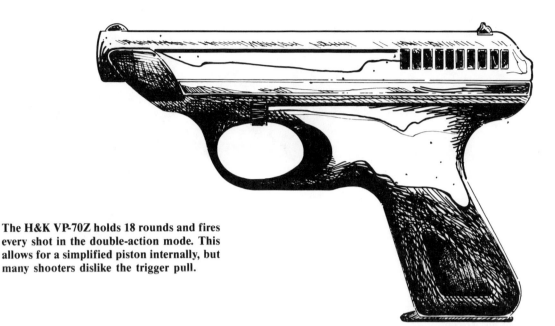

The H&K VP-70Z holds 18 rounds and fires every shot in the double-action mode. This allows for a simplified piston internally, but many shooters dislike the trigger pull.

the grip base; this is especially poor when using the pistol in the burst mode, since it can go through magazines quite quickly. Some of the drawbacks of this placement are overcome, however, with the VP-70's large 18-round magazine.

The front sight presents both good and bad news for the shooter. The front sight is a double wing arrangement similar to the rear sight; the shooter lines up the space in the front sight with the space in the rear sight, which gives a good sight picture in a wide variety of light conditions. However, it also creates a wide front sight which many shooters find covers up the target at longer ranges—and the whole idea of a stocked weapon is long-range accuracy.

Some shooters love the VP-70; many other shooters, however, despise it as a combat weapon. Shooters should try one out before making a decision one way or the other. It does offer a lot of bang for the buck and its simple design makes maintenance easy.

Field-stripping is quite simple. Remove the magazine and cycle the pistol to be sure it's empty; release the slide release inside the trigger guard under the frame; pull the slide to the rear and then up and allow it to run forward off the frame. Reassembly is the reverse of this procedure.

Specifications

Overall length: 8 inches
             (21.5 inches with stock)
Weight (unloaded): 2.5 lbs. (3.5 lbs. with stock)

Barrel length: 4.57 inches
Magazine capacity: 18

IVER JOHNSON 9MM PISTOL

This all-steel pistol is a spinoff of Iver Johnson's Pony pistol. It follows the basic design of the Browning 1911-A1, but is much smaller and uses a double-action trigger. The pistol has an adjustable rear sight and hardwood grip plates. Finishes are blue or a less reflective matte blue.

The Iver Johnson pistol was unavailable for testing at the time of this writing but certainly merits consideration as a very small 9mm pistol which could be an ideal back-up/hide-away gun. Field-stripping is nearly identical to that of the 1911-A1.

Specifications

Overall length: 6.5 inches
Weight (unloaded): 1.63 lbs.
Barrel length: 3 inches
Magazine capacity: 6

KASSNAR MBK-9HP

This MBK-9HP is imported by Kassnar Imports. The pistol may be encountered under other names in the near future.

The pistol is made by Fegyver in Budapest, Hungary. Hungary, especially since its communist takeover, has never been noted for originality in

The Iver Johnson 9mm pistol is an all-steel spin-off of their Pony pistol. It follows the basic design details of the Browning 1911-A1 but is much smaller and uses a double-action trigger. The pistol's small size merits consideration for those looking for a very small 9mm pistol. Photo courtesy of Iver Johnson.

pistol making, and this pistol is no exception. It is styled after the Browning Hi-Power complete with the 9mm Luger chambering.

Internally, there are a few differences from the Hi-Power, the most noticeable being a double-action trigger and the P-38 style hammer-drop safety that most new 9mm pistols now sport. The Hungarian design has also done away with the Hi-Power's magazine disconnector safety. The frame and slide are made of blued steel. Unfortunately the pistol doesn't have an internal firing-pin safety, so it's not all that safe to carry with the safety off and a round in the chamber.

The pistol is relatively inexpensive compared to many other 9mm pistols. However, if a shooter wants a double-action weapon patterned off the Hi-Power, probably the new Browning double-action pistol would be worth spending a little extra money for.

Takedown is nearly identical to the Browning, as are most of the size/weight specifications.

KORRIPHILA HSP 701

The Korriphila pistols are custom made by Edgar Budichowsky in Heidelberg, Germany, to the specifications of the buyers: caliber (any of ten), trigger action (single, double, selective fire), barrel length, finish, safety placement, etc., can all be chosen according to specific desires. While these pistols are well designed and incorporate a single-roller lockup system devised by Budichowsky, their single-column magazines and $1,200-plus price tag make them unsuitable for most combat needs. Unless you're living the part of the *Man with the Golden Gun,* you'd probably be better off with a Beretta, Smith & Wesson, or Browning.

LLAMA 1911 LOOK-ALIKES

The Llama pistols are manufactured by Gabilondo y Compania, which dates back to 1904. The company produced pistols for the French in World War I and a variety of automatics during the 1930s patterned after the Browning 1910 and sold under the names of "Ruby," "Danton," and "Buffalo."

In 1931 Gabilondo started producing a series of pistols which borrowed greatly from the Colt 1911-A1, with the major differences being parts size and elimination of the Colt grip safety. The pistols made for larger calibers used a Browning-style locking system, while models made for smaller calibers fired from blowback. These pistols became known as the Llama pistols though some export models have the importing company's name on them.

The Llama 9mm Luger "Colt" pistols have little to recommend them; other more modern handguns are better suited for combat. Too, many of the Llama pistols are very finicky about ammunition, seem prone to problems, and often have less than

These Llama pistols date back to 1931 when Gabilondo started producing a series of pistols which borrowed greatly from the Colt 1911-A1. These pistols use a Browning-style locking system, while models made for smaller calibers are fired from blowback. Photo courtesy of Stoeger Industries.

flawless fit and finish. The pistols do come in a number of chamberings for those who want a family of pistols. The "Small Frame" pistols are available in .22 LR, .32 ACP, and .380 ACP, while the "Large Frame" models come in .45 ACP, 9mm Luger, and .38 Super.

Because of the mirror finish on many blued Llamas, the satin nickel finish is generally more ideal for a combat pistol.

LLAMA OMNI

The Omni was the pistol which Llama hoped would capture the large-capacity, double-action automatic market. In the U.S. at least, the pistol was less than successful. Though its ball-bearing hammer spring, double sear bars (one for single action, the other for double), buttress rifling, and

"prebroken" firing pin (which, according to company literature, has a ball joint where firing pins normally break) all sounded good, the pistols didn't deliver on the promises as far as many shooters were concerned. Too, the pistols were introduced before the 9mm Luger cartridge started to gain acceptance in the U.S.

The Omni pistol was made both in 9mm and .45 ACP. Llama announced its discontinuance in 1985. The pistol will be replaced by the Llama 82, a high-capacity 9mm automatic which is the standard Spanish Army sidearm. The new pistol was unavailable for testing at the time of this writing.

Specifications

Overall length: 8 inches (7.75 inches, .45)
Weight (unloaded): 2.5 lbs.

Barrel length: 4.25 inches
Magazine capacity: 13 rounds (7 rounds in .45)

MAS

The French rejected the Browning Hi-Power in favor of an inferior pistol, the 1935A, designed by Charles Gabriel Petter. This pistol proved hard to manufacture and was saddled with an anemic .30-caliber French round. In an effort to speed up production, a simplified version was created; this slab-sided monstrosity was called the 1935S. (Interestingly, when the Nazis invaded France, the French stopped production of the weapon rather than continuing to make the pistols for use by the Germans.)

Following World War II, the Petter pistol was reworked for 9mm Luger and in 1948 was adopted by the French as the Mle 1950. Unfortunately, the awkward slide-mounted safety was not lost in the design shuffle and magazine capacity was only nine pounds. Consequently, this pistol has little to offer and has several serious design faults.

PARABELLUM ("LUGER")

Perhaps the most famous of the 9mm Luger weapons is, perhaps understandably, the "Luger." This weapon was introduced in 1900 and was quickly purchased by German officers. It may have seen action as early as the Boxer Rebellion of 1901.

The weapon is officially known as the Parabellum. An American importer, A. F. Stoeger, noticed that the pistols were commonly called "Lugers" in the U.S. and elsewhere. Thus, in 1923 he registered the name "Luger" and marketed the pistols he imported with the name. In 1970, the Stoeger Company started making rough .22 LR copies of the original Luger pistols. Although these are completely different, the .22 is legally a real "Luger" since it is made by the company that owns the rights to the name!

The Parabellum was perfected by the Austrian Georg Luger. Most of his pistols were manufactured at the Deutsche Waffen und Munitionsfabrik in Berlin, Germany. The weapon was not totally new; it was a redesigned Borchardt pistol to which DWM owned the rights and which had been manufactured as early as 1893. The reworking created a swan from an ugly duckling; the Para-

bellum pistol is still considered by many to be one of the best-looking handguns ever made. Several manufacturers continue to make the weapon to the present day, with variants chambered for a number of other rounds including .22 LR and .30 Luger.

The weapon was adopted by the Swiss Army in 1901 and remained the standard sidearm until 1948. The weapon was also adopted by the militaries of Bulgaria, Brazil, Chile, Germany, the Netherlands, and Portugal.

The U.S. military came close to adopting the Parabellum twice—once in .30 Luger and once in .45 ACP. During field tests of the .30-caliber pistols around 1901, they proved prone to jamming, however, and thus were not adopted. The 700 to 1,000 "American Eagle" Parabellums purchased for tests were finally sold as military surplus between 1906 and 1910.

In 1907, the Army requested pistols and revolvers for testing in .45. DMW submitted two or three pistols in this chambering for trials. Like many other pistols, the Parabellum proved to be inferior to the Browning/Colt and Savage.

The Parabellum pistols fared better in Europe, though not a whole lot better. While the Parabellum remained an alternate choice for German officers during World War II, the Germans dropped the Parabellum in favor of the P-38 for a number of good reasons. While it points well, the Parabellum often has a poor trigger pull, and is sensitive to dirt and choosy about ammunition. These last two points often cause it to jam in battle. The Parabellum was not (and is not) the first choice as a combat weapon.

In addition to DWM, the Luger has been manufactured by the Mauser and Krieghoff factories in Germany, as well as by the Swiss in Bern and even the English, who made Parabellum pistols for the Dutch military for a short time. An endless variety of Parabellums has been manufactured, and refinishing/rebuilding following World War I created a number of half breeds. Some of the more common types are:

1. The 1900 or "Old Model" Parabellum adopted by the Swiss and later the German navy. This version is distinguished by its dished toggle knobs, toggle lock, and laminated recoil spring. Its safety is located on the back of its grip.

2. The 1906 or "New Model" Parabellum has a coiled recoil spring and no toggle lock. The toggle knobs are checkered and it has a grip safety similar to the Old Model.

The Parabellum pistol, despite its mystique and legend, is expensive to manufacture. While it points well, the weapon is often cursed with a poor trigger pull and is sensitive to dirt and choosy about ammunition. These last two failings cause it to jam when used extensively in battle. The Parabellum is not the first choice as a combat weapon.

3. The P.08 German Army model has no grip safety and often has a detachable stock lug.

4. The "Artillery Model" was created from the basic P.08. It had a longer barrel with sights mounted ahead of the receiver and could be easily fired like a rifle when the detachable stock was mounted. A special 32-round snail magazine was also developed for this version. In the U.S., a metal and leather holster/stock was created for the Parabellum by the American Ideal Holster Company around 1900. The Swiss experimented with a 16-round magazine/wooden stocked Parabellum around 1908.

5. The Model 1929 was created by the Swiss in an effort to keep manufacturing costs down. These pistols work well, but have a rougher finish and

This P.08 German Army model of the Luger is without grip safety and was often made with a detachable stock slot cut into its grip. This pistol probably saw use in World War II, and is now among the war trophies of an American GI.

lack checkering in many areas including the toggle knob, safety button, magazine release, and takedown lever. The 1929 has a grip safety.

While the Parabellum pistols are attractive firearms, they aren't ideal for combat given the large number of other suitable pistols. Many of the best Parabellums are collector's items, while many of those available are built from surplus parts of dubious origin and quality.

RADOM (VIS) 1935

The Radom was designed in 1935 by Piotr Wilniewczyc and Jan Skrzypinski in Radom, Poland, with the help of FN technicians. The pistol differs from the Hi-Power in a number of ways. It has much in common with the Browning/Colt 1911 automatic pistol. Early models often had a detachable shoulder stock, but this was soon dispensed with.

The Radom has the dubious 1911-style grip safety and omits the thumb safety (the pistol was to be carried with the hammer down, then cocked

when brought into use—hardly safe by modern standards). The pistol has an 8-round magazine and hammer release lever, which is often mistaken for a manual safety, so that the user can safely lower the hammer with one hand. This lever is located on the left side of the slide and moves the firing pin out of the reach before releasing the hammer.

When the Nazi Army overran Poland in 1939, Radom pistols were manufactured for Nazi use. Many of these pistols were sabotaged, so any Radom bearing Nazi proof marks should be carefully examined to be sure it is safe to fire. Many pistols made during this period do not have the stock slot or hammer release mechanism.

While the Radom design is very tough and was certainly good for its time, the lack of spare parts and limited magazine capacity make it a poor choice as a modern self-defense weapon.

RUGER P-85

Sturm, Ruger & Company, Inc., has recently perfected the design of its 9mm pistol, the Ruger

The Sturm, Ruger P-85 promises to capture a large share of the combat pistol market, thanks to a low price brought about by good design and modern manufacturing techniques. The pistol has an ambidextrous safety and magazine release, along with a 15-round magazine. Photo courtesy of Sturm, Ruger & Company, Inc.

Field-stripping the P-85 can be carried out with a minimum of trouble and no tools. Photo courtesy of Sturm, Ruger & Company, Inc.

P-85, which is slated for release toward the end of 1986. If other Ruger products are any indication, this pistol will probably become very popular thanks to good engineering, which takes advantage of modern manufacturing methods and materials. Projected price for this promising pistol will be *very* competitive with other pistols currently on the combat pistol market.

The P-85 has few features which are unique; rather, like most modern firearms, it "borrows" the good features from other weapons and incorporates them in a superior firearm. The pistol has both an ambidextrous safety and magazine release. A safety lever and rectangular magazine-release button are found on each side of the pistol. The releases themselves are placed at the rear of the trigger guard where most feel it is most convenient for quick reloading of the 15-round magazine. Like most other modern pistols, the P-85 has a safety which disengages the trigger mechanism from the trigger and blocks the firing pin.

The rear sight is drift-adjustable for windage, and the front sight is staked with double roll pins to prevent it from coming loose with extended firing. Both front and rear sights have white dot inserts to aid in sighting.

The exposed hammer spur is of the burr style and grooved on top to allow for single-action firing of the first shot if the shooter so desires. Normally, the double-action trigger would probably be employed for a quick first shot. Following the first shot, the weapon fires in the single-action mode as is common with most modern pistols.

The P-85's frame is an aluminum alloy with a matte black finish; the slide is chrome-molybdenum steel with a similar finish. Made of tough plastic, the grips have wide grooves molded into the plastic to give the shooter a good grip in adverse weather conditions. The slide has an extra large ejection port to help prevent "stove pipe" jams.

Ruger has chosen to use a tilting-barrel, link-locking system similar to that of the Browning/Colt .45 with a recoil spring/guide rod located below the barrel. Takedown appears to be similar to that of the Browning Hi-Power.

Although the P-85 was unavailable for testing at the time of this writing, the manufacturer has tested prototype guns with 10,000 round firings without any damage or obvious wear to the pistols.

Specifications

Overall length: 7.84 inches
Weight (unloaded): 2 lbs.
Barrel length: 4.5 inches
Magazine capacity: 15

SCHWEIZERISCHE INDUSTRIE GESELLSCHAFT (SIG) PISTOLS

The SIG SP46/8 was based on the French 1935A pistol. The 1935A had an ill-conceived safety placed near the top of its slide and was saddled with a weak round. The Swiss alleviated this problem by enlarging the weapon to handle 9mm Luger and by replacing the slide safety with one on the frame.

SIG also did away with the barrel links used to lock the action during recoil and instead used a camming ramp on the barrel lug. The slide rails were also lengthened and made so that the slide rides inside the top of the frame.

With these major changes, the SIG SP47/8 became a good combat pistol and was adopted by the Swiss, Danish, and the German border police.

SIG P210

When the Swiss adopted the SP47/8 as their military pistol in 1949, it was designated the P210; it continued in service until 1975. SIG continues to make the popular pistol for commercial sales. Except for the magazine release located on the bottom of the pistol grip and the limited magazine capacity, the pistol is very well designed.

The P210 can be converted to 7.62mm Luger by changing the barrel and recoil spring. A .22 LR conversion unit is also available as a training aid.

Field-stripping is similar to that of other Browning-style pistols. Remove the magazine and cycle the weapon to be sure it's empty; pull the slide back a half inch to line up the disassembly notch in the slide with the slide release; push out the slide release lever from right to left of the receiver; release the slide and allow it to run forward off the frame; carefully push the recoil spring and rod toward the front of the slide to release and lift the spring and rod out; and remove the barrel. It is also possible to remove the hammer/disconnector, sear, and mainspring assembly by pulling the ham-

9MM AND .38 SUPER   75

mer up out of the frame. Reassembly is a reversal of this procedure. If the firing pin needs to be replaced, it can be removed by depressing its back slightly and removing the plate that holds it up and out of the slide. Be careful, as the firing pin is spring-loaded and may "fire" out of the back of the slide when released.

Specifications

Overall length: 8.5 inches
Weight (unloaded): 2.14 lbs.
Barrel length: 4.72 inches
Magazine capacity: 8

SIG-SAUER P220

The SIG-Sauer P220 was designed around the SIG P210 as a joint effort of SIG and J. P. Sauer & Hohn of West Germany. The guns are manufactured at the Sauer factory in Eckernforde.

The P220 has a double-action trigger and a firing-pin block which allows it to be safely carried without a thumb safety or similar device. The decocking lever is at the upper front of the left grip panel; on the P-220, when the decocking lever is pulled down, the hammer falls to half cock rather than all the way down. The magazine release is located at the grip base, and the disassembly lever on the left side of the frame slightly over and in front of the trigger. The slide lock/release is located on the top rear of the left grip plate and is rather awkward. Interestingly, barrel lockup is achieved with the barrel against the rear of the ejection port. This allows the barrel to be made without barrel lugs or cuts. Never alter the rear of the ejection port on these pistols or the lockup will be weakened. An alloy frame reduces the overall weight. The pistol is available in 9mm Luger, 7.65 Luger, .38 Super, and .45 ACP. Like the P210, this pistol has a .22 LR adapter for training use.

Field-stripping is simple. Remove the magazine and cycle the slide to be sure the weapon is empty; pull the slide back and lock it open; rotate the disassembly lever down; release the slide while holding it and ease it forward off the frame; and remove the recoil spring and guide along with the barrel. Reassembly is a reversal of this procedure.

Specifications

Overall length: 7.81 inches
Weight (unloaded): 1.8 lbs.
Barrel length: 4.38 inches
Magazine capacity: 8 (7 in .45 ACP)

SIG-SAUER P225

The P225 is an aluminum-framed, chopped version of the P220 created in 1975 to capture some of the market for a handgun which didn't require operating a safety before being fired. The Germans designated the P225 as the P6 and adopted it as the standard pistol for a number of their police forces.

Some P225s are cursed with a magazine release located at the bottom of the pistol grip. Most, however, are mounted on the left side of the pistol grip behind the trigger guard, a very good feature for a small-capacity pistol.

Like other short-barreled 9mm pistols, the P225 is a bit less accurate than many longer-barreled pistols and is somewhat of a fire-breather with some brands of ammunition.

Specifications

Overall length: 7 inches
Weight (unloaded): 1.8 lbs.
Barrel length: 3.84 inches
Magazine capacity: 8

SIG-SAUER P226

The P226 is similar to the P225 but has a double-row magazine; this increased magazine capacity was created with only slightly more than a tenth of an inch increase in the grip width. The pistol is also blessed with a magazine release on the side of the pistol grip.

The P226 was apparently created in an effort to win the U.S. military pistol contract. The P226 was submitted by Maremont Corporation, which had acquired the U.S. manufacturing and marketing rights. The P226 performed very well in the trials and more or less tied the Beretta 92SB-F as the winner. The P226 was more expensive to make, however, so the Beretta was adopted. Like the Beretta, the P226 is very reliable with a wide range of ammunition. Many P226 pistols show a slight preference for CCI's 115-grain "Blazer" ammunition when it comes to accuracy, though P226 accuracy is good with a variety of ammunition. Although the magazine catch can be reversed for left-handed shooters, the hammer-lowering lever is awkward and the magazine release impossible to reach for southpaws.

The P 226 is probably one of the best combat pistols in 9mm Luger and is being adopted by a number of law-enforcement agencies in the U.S. and Canada.

To field-strip, remove the magazine and cycle the weapon to be sure it's empty; pull the slide back; lock the slide open by pushing the slide release up; rotate the disassembly lever down on the left of the frame; release slide release lever and take the slide off; and remove the recoil spring, rod, and barrel. Reassembly is a reversal of this procedure.

Specifications

Overall length: 7.75 inches
Weight (unloaded): 1.94 lbs.
Barrel length: 3.38 inches
Magazine capacity: 15

SMITH & WESSON MODEL 39

In 1949 the U.S. military was thinking about switching to a lightweight 9mm Luger pistol; while this turned out to be a false start, it did lead to the production of the Model 39 automatic by Smith & Wesson.

This pistol was created with a lower frame of aluminum alloy coated with a black finish. The pistol has a magazine disconnector safety (which can be easily removed by a competent gunsmith). The overall design was based on the Browning Hi-Power (especially the barrel lockup) coupled with the hammer drop and trigger mechanism of the P-38. Unlike many modern hammer-drop safeties, that of the S&W 39 does not have an internal trigger-coupled firing-pin safety; therefore, this pistol should not be carried with the hammer down and the safety off.

The S&W 39 does have two problem points. One is a feed ramp with a hump in it that makes some types of bullet shapes get hung up during chambering. This hump can easily be smoothed out by a gunsmith. The second shortcoming is a narrow extractor which sometimes fails to extract rounds, especially if the chamber is dirty.

To field strip, remove the magazine and cycle the pistol to be sure it's empty; place safety in the upper (fire) position; pull the slide back until the disassembly notch on the left of the slide lines up with the slide release lever; push out the slide release lever from right to left of the receiver; move the slide forward and off the frame; carefully push the recoil spring and rod toward the front of the slide to release and lift the spring and rod out; rotate the barrel bushing to the left side of the slide and pull it out of the slide; remove the barrel. Reassembly is a reversal of this procedure; be careful to push the sear release spur on the rear of the frame down when putting the slide back on the frame.

Specifications

Overall length: 7.44 inches
Weight (unloaded): 1.66 lbs.
Barrel length: 4 inches
Magazine capacity: 8

SMITH & WESSON 59

The Model 59 is basically a Model 39 with a double-row magazine. Unfortunately, like the 39, it cannot be carried with complete safety with the hammer down and the thumb safety off. This really defeats the convenience of a double-action trigger. Coupled with this problem are a lot of stories of poor reliability, so that sales have not been as great as they might have been.

SMITH & WESSON 439/639

The 439 is the updated version of the S&W 39 and corrects most of its shortcomings. It has an automatic firing-pin block, so the pistol can be carried with the hammer down and the safety off. The extractor is wider and the feed ramp straighter.

The only problem with this pistol is that it has its parent gun's limited capacity. The aluminum alloy frame is still used in a blue or nickel finish. In addition to the standard fixed sight, a micrometer click sight is available which is adjustable for windage and elevation. An ambidextrous safety has also been added to the new model. A satin finish, stainless-steel version is also being marketed as the 639. The 639 weighs six ounces more than the alloy frame 439.

The Smith & Wesson 439 is the updated version of the S&W 39. The 439 corrects most of the shortcomings of the 39 with its automatic firing-pin block and a wider extractor. The only problem with this pistol is that it has the limited capacity of its parent gun. Photo courtesy of Smith & Wesson.

The Smith & Wesson 639 is the stainless-steel updated version of the S&W 39. Like other new S&W automatics, this pistol has an internal firing-pin block and a wider extractor. Photo courtesy of Smith & Wesson.

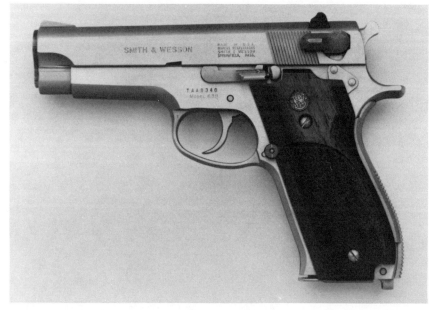

Takedown and specifications for the 439/639 are nearly identical to that of the 39. It should be noted that the disassembly of this and other newer S&W automatics often requires a soft mallet and drift punch to remove the slide stop, which can be quite tight on new pistols.

SMITH & WESSON 459/659

Like the 39/439, the 59 was updated to become the 459 in the early 1980s. The new model is blessed with an automatic firing-pin block, so the pistol can be carried with the hammer down and the safety off. This, coupled with a 14-round magazine and an ambidextrous safety, makes it an excellent combat weapon. Like the 439/639, the pistol enjoys an improved feeding ramp and wider extractor.

A slightly modified 459, the 459M, was entered in the JSSAP trials to select a new U.S. service arm. The most noticeable differences are the 459M's enlarged, squared-off trigger guard and fixed sights. Internally, the weapon lacks the magazine disconnector, a welcome change. The 459M proved slightly less desirable than the Beretta and SIG-Sauer, however, and the pistol was not adopted.

The 459 has an aluminum alloy frame with either a blue or nickel finish. In addition to the standard fixed sight, a micrometer "click" sight adjustable for windage and elevation is available.

The 459 pistol has an alloy frame to cut down on its weight and a blued finish. It has a standard 14-round magazine and is available with either fixed rear sight or fully adjustable target sights. Photo courtesy of Smith & Wesson.

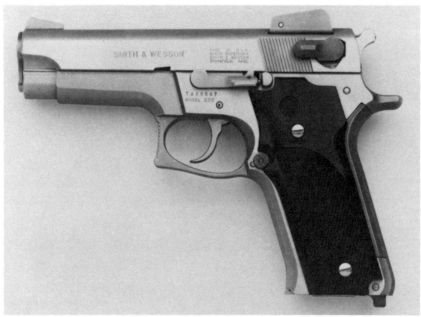

The 659 is the stainless-steel version of the 459 pistol. With a satin finish, it weighs 9.5 ounces more than the alloy-frame 459. In addition to the standard 14-round magazine designed for this pistol, a 20-round magazine is also available. Photo courtesy of Smith & Wesson.

A satin finish, stainless steel version is available as the 659; it weighs 9.5 ounces more than the alloy frame 459. In addition to the standard 14-round magazine, a 20-round magazine is available.

Takedown is nearly identical to that of the 39.

Specifications

Overall length: 7.63 inches
Weight (unloaded): 1.88 lbs. (659, 2.47 lbs.)
Barrel length: 4 inches
Magazine capacity: 14

SMITH & WESSON 469/669

In 1983, a chopped version of the 459 was introduced by Smith & Wesson. For some time, similar weapons were being custom created by gunsmiths from S&W 39s, 439s, 59s, etc., but such alteration voided Smith & Wesson's warranty. The new 469 had all the pluses and none of the liabilities as a hide-away gun.

The weapon has its own 12-round magazine with an extended finger hook, but will also accept the 14-round or 20-round 459 magazines. Only the fixed rear sight is available on this model; the sight is dehorned to give it snag-free performance. The

The S&W 469, a chopped version of the 459, was introduced in 1983. The weapon has a 12-round magazine but will also accept the 14-round or 20-round 459 magazines. The pistol has been "dehorned" to give it snagfree performance. With an internal firing-pin safety, this pistol makes an ideal hideout pistol. Photo courtesy of Smith & Wesson.

The S&W 669 is the stainless version of the 469. The magazine well is slightly beveled to aid magazine insertion, and the barrel is hard-chromed to increase bore life and aid in cleaning. The 669 model has a stainless-steel slide and an alloy frame, both with a nonglare finish. Photo courtesy of Smith & Wesson.

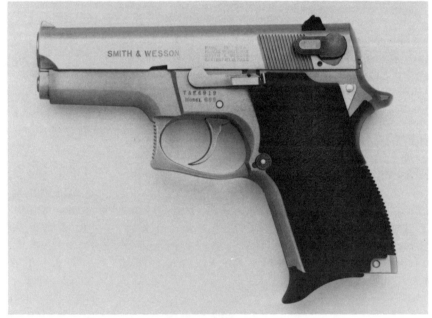

hammer is bobbed (but grooved on top for thumb cocking), the grip panels thinned and pebbled, and the grip spur shortened to aid in concealment. The magazine well is slightly beveled to aid magazine insertion. The barrel is hard-chromed to increase bore life and aid in cleaning.

The 469 is the alloy frame, blued version of the chopped pistol while the 669 model has a stainless steel slide and an alloy frame with a nonglare finish. Occasionally, satin-plated pistols are made by S&W on special order. (The shooter should be sure S&W has done the work if he is concerned about warranty of the pistol.)

Winchester Silvertips usually give good perfor-

mance in the 469/669 pistols while Federal 115 JHP's give the best accuracy, though the pistol works well with a wide range of ammunition.

Disassembly is identical to other S&W autos except that a belled muzzle on the barrel has done away with the barrel bushing.

Specifications

Overall length: 6.81 inches
Weight (unloaded): 1.63 lbs.
Barrel length: 3.5 inches
Magazine capacity: 12

STAR MODEL A/M

The Star line of pistols was introduced in 1921 by Star Bonifacio Echeverria, S.A., of Eibar; it was based on the Colt/Browning designs. Only one model, the Modelo 1921, had a grip safety. Later models have avoided it as it met with disfavor with military testers.

Early Star pistols were chambered for 7.63mm Mauser, 9mm Largo, .38 ACP, and .45 ACP. They included selective-fire models with the usual detachable shoulder stock. During World War II, Star pistols made in 9mm Luger were purchased by many other countries as the Model A. In a nearly uncontrollable selective-fire version, the Star was known as the Model M. Later a slightly modified version of the Model A, the Star Super, replaced both earlier pistols.

STAR MODEL BM

The Star Model BM was adopted by Spanish military and paramilitary forces for a time. This pistol looks like a 1911-A1 without a grip safety. Unlike the Colt, the Star has a magazine disconnector safety and a thumb safety that locks the slide when the hammer is down. The blued version is suitable for combat; the brilliant chrome version with pearlite grips is probably better left in a display cabinet. The BKM model is an alloy frame BM. Mercifully, it is not available in the chromed version.

Because of their limited magazine capacity, these weapons are not a first choice for combat except as a 9mm pistol which operates nearly identically to the Colt.

STAR MODEL 28

Star pistols have evolved away from their "Browning look," so that newer models actually are quite different. The Model 28 and the later Model 30 have gained a reputation for reliability and are greatly liked by many shooters.

The Model 28 double-action pistol was introduced in 1980 and was among the early entries in the U.S. military pistol contract contest. However, as the tests were delayed, the Star 28 dropped out of the running.

The pistol uses a modified Hi-Power locking system, has a slide-mounted ambidextrous thumb safety, and a burr/ring hammer. Most pistols have a dark phosphate finish. The Model 28 uses no screws; a tool is needed only to adjust its sights. Unfortunately, it is also blessed with a magazine disconnector safety. The hammer can be left back with the thumb safety on for cock and lock carry.

To field-strip, remove the magazine and cycle the weapon to be sure it's empty; pull the slide back so that the disassembly guide marks on the left side of the frame and slide line up; push out the slide release lever from right to left of the receiver; release the slide and allow it to run forward off the frame; carefully push the recoil spring and rod toward the front of the slide to release and lift the spring and rod out; finally, remove the barrel. If there is a need to do so, the uncocked hammer/backstrap/hammer spring can be removed by depressing the plunger in the backstrap of the grip. Reassembly is the reversal of this procedure.

Specifications

Overall length: 8.1 inches
Weight (unloaded): 2.38 lbs.
Barrel length: 4.33 inches
Magazine capacity: 15

STAR MODEL 30

This is a slightly modified Model 28 whose most notable change is a beefed up extractor. The 30PK is an alloy frame, slightly shorter barrel/slide model; the 30M is the standard steel frame version. Both have plastic grip plates.

The rear sight is adjustable for windage. The trigger is grooved, which some find objectionable since it hampers the trigger finger's slide from a double- to single-action pull. A loaded chamber indicator is also included. On some pistols the magazine release is quite stiff and should be reworked by a gunsmith.

As with the Model 28, many people in need of a combat pistol find the Star Model 30 to their liking.

STEYR GB

The Roth-Steyr was one of the first self-loading pistols to be used by a major European army; the Austro-Hungarian cavalry started carrying it in 1907. By 1912 the Steyr company was producing the Model 1912 Steyr Hahn automatic

The Steyr GB is gas operated and feeds from a double-row magazine similar to that of a rifle. The pistol has dispensed with external safeties and has a hammer drop lever in the position on the slide normally occupied by a manual safety; through the use of internal, automatic safeties, the pistol is nearly as easy to use as a revolver but has a lot more firepower—18 rounds in the magazine. Photo courtesy of Gun South.

in a 9mm chambering slightly less powerful than the 9mm Luger. The pistol was a sort of cross between the Roth-Steyr and the Browning 1900 and was available with a detachable stock.

After the German takeover of Austria before World War II, many of the 1912 pistols were rechambered for 9mm Luger. These pistols are marked "P-08." The 1912's action is quite strong and safe to use with the more powerful chambering.

Following World War II, Steyr made a version of the Walther P-38 for the Austrian army. When the army decided to adopt a new pistol, Steyr started work on one. The new pistol, the Steyr GB, was developed during the 1970s. It uses a double-action trigger which releases the internal trigger-block safety and has no manual safeties. This allows the gun to be brought into action quickly and safely carried with the hammer down.

The Steyr FB was first offered in a selective-fire version with an extended 36-round magazine

and a detachable stock which doubled as a holster. The selector was placed in the slide position occupied by the hammer drop lever. Steyr seems to have shelved this version due to lack of interest.

The pistol is potentially more accurate than many other 9mm Luger pistols since it has a fixed barrel. The locking mechanism is created by bleeding gas from the barrel to retard the slide, hence the "GB": *"Gazbremse"* or gas brake. Early pistols were also designated the "Pi 18," apparently a reference to the magazine capacity. The barrel looks quite different from most, with a gas hole in its top and two rings on a large hump just behind the gas port. Inside, the barrel has polygonal rifling, which means that the bullet is deformed during firing and then twisted by the uneven spiraling inside diameter of the barrel. This stabilizes the bullet well and has the added benefit of making cleaning very easy. Also, for those who practice with lead bullets, the barrel doesn't lead as easily as do those barrels with lands and grooves.

The barrel is hard-chromed inside and out to aid in cleaning and extend its life.

An added plus of the gas system is that it seems to buffer recoil somewhat. Many shooters feel the pistol is easier to keep on target when firing multiple shots.

What appears to be a slide safety on the left rear of the slide is actually the hammer-lowering mechanism. After use, it springs back into place, leaving an internal hammer-block safety in place; when the trigger is pulled, this internal safety is automatically released. This makes a lot more sense than the hammer drop/safety, which must be manually placed into the fire position. Unfortunately, most GB pistols don't have an ambidextrous hammer drop; left-handed users will need two hands to lower the hammer.

The frame and slide are made of steel, and luminous dots are placed on the front and rear sights. The frame is covered with a crackle finish which isn't pretty but is durable. The slide has a more conventional finish with blued sides and matte finish top. The slide release is a bit large; shooters using a two-hand grip need to be careful not to activate it accidentally. The grips and trigger guard are made of grooved and checkered plastic; shooters with small hands may also find the grip a bit large.

The Steyr GB also has a large magazine; with a round in the chamber, a shooter has 19 rounds available, and with the magazine release conveniently placed at the rear of the trigger guard and a slide release, quick reloading is possible. The magazine is a double feed; rounds feed alternately from the left and right.

A slightly modified GB was entered into the U.S. JSSAP tests. This pistol had an ambidextrous hammer drop, a lanyard loop, a metal finger guard rather than the standard plastic, and a parkerized matte finish on both frame and slide.

The Steyr GB is an excellent combat pistol which functions well with a wide range of ammunition. It should be considered by anyone who needs a large-capacity 9mm pistol.

Takedown is fairly simple: remove the magazine and make sure the pistol is empty; rotate the disassembly lever down; rotate the front barrel bushing counterclockwise; slide out the bushing and recoil spring guide; lift the slide off the frame. Reassembly is a reversal of this procedure.

Specifications

Overall length: 8.5 inches
Weight (unloaded): 2.2 lbs.
Barrel length: 5.4 inches
Magazine capacity: 18

TAURUS PT 92/99

In 1980 Forjas Taurus took over the Brazilian Beretta factory in São Paulo. Part of the understanding of the takeover was that Taurus could produce the Beretta Series 92 pistols with the machinery in the plant but that the Beretta name could not be used and Taurus could not compete with Beretta on some world markets.

Taurus produced the standard 92, many of which were exported to the U.S. for a short period, but soon modified the design slightly. The Taurus 92 is now somewhat of a cross between the 92S and 92F. The ambidextrous frame-mounted safety was retained, while the magazine release was moved behind the trigger guard. The trigger guard was squared off and grooves were placed on the front and back of the grip. The lower front of the grip keeps the same straight slant of the 92S. Internally, a firing-pin block was added so that the pin is unable to reach the cartridge until the trigger is fully retracted; this allows safe carrying with the hammer down and the safety off or with the safety on and the hammer cocked.

There are currently four models of the Taurus 92 automatic: the standard PT-92, a chopped PT-92 designated the "Mini PT 92" in the U.S., the PT-99, with adjustable rear sight, and the PT-99 with a satin nickel finish. All four have non-checkered walnut grips. (Because Brazilian laws forbid the ownership of 9mm Luger firearms by citizens, a blowback copy is also made in .32 ACP. This might be of use as a training aid, but its size is too large for consideration as a combat weapon. This pistol is designated as the PT-57. Many shooters feel that Taurus pistols are not as high in quality as Beretta pistols made in the U.S. and Italy. However, this seems to be changing, and the Taurus pistols are often available with a lower price tag than their Beretta counterparts.

Field-stripping and specifications of the PT-92/99 are identical to those for the Beretta 92.

TUL'SKIY TOKAREV 30/33

The TT30 and TT33 pistols are chambered for a special Russian cartridge that is slightly weaker than the 9mm Luger or .38 Super. This is the 7.62mm Tokarev, which is nearly identical to the 7.63mm Mauser. In the West, the Soviet cartridges are rare, but can be reloaded to 7.63mm Mauser specifications.

The TT30 and TT33 have become very important to a number of Eastern Bloc countries. Poland, Hungary, and Yugoslavia produce the pistols as the M48, China as the Type 51 and Type 54, and North Korea as the M68. Yugoslavia makes a 9mm Luger version designated the M65. The pistol has also been produced in a modified form by Egypt as the Tokagypt 58.

While the TT30/TT33 pistols are no longer in use in the Soviet military, many of the pistols have been exported, and other countries make copies of the pistol.

The pistols are far from original. The action is an unblushing copy of the Colt/Browning 1911-A1 automatic design, complete with swinging locking link and barrel locking lugs. However, some new features were also added to simplify manufacture and maintenance: the sear/hammer mechanism can be removed for, cleaning, the barrel magazine guide lips are machined into the pistol itself, and the grip and manual safeties have been done away with. The TT33 appears to have been created by simplifying the manufacturing process and has little to distinguish it externally. Internally, the barrel lugs are cut around the barrel rather than just in its top, and other simplifications are also to be found.

There is a little confusion in the West as to how many versions of the Tokarev exist. It appears that there are at least two major versions, the TT30 and TT33, along with the R3, a .22 training pistol, and the TTR4 or R4, a .22 target pistol with extra long barrel and adjustable sights.

The Tul'skiy Tokarev 33 pistol is far from original. Its action is an unblushing copy of the Colt/Browning 1911-A1 automatic design, complete with swinging locking link and barrel locking lugs. However, some new features were also added to simplify both manufacture and maintenance: the sear/hammer mechanism can be removed for cleaning; the barrel magazine guide lips are machined into the pistol itself, and the grip and manual safeties have been done away with (something that wouldn't even be considered in the West).

The TT30 has become very important to a number of Eastern Bloc countries with Poland, Hungary, and Yugoslavia producing the pistols (as their M48); China produces copies as its Type 51 and Type 54, and North Korea, as its M68. Yugoslavia makes a version in 9mm Luger designated the M65. The pistol has also been produced in a modified form by Egypt as the "Tokagypt 58."

The TT30/TT33 is a simple pistol with all the reliability of the Browning type. Unfortunately, it is chambered for a poor combat cartridge and lacks a reliable safety. All in all, this is not an ideal weapon.

Field-stripping is similar to that of most Browning-style pistols. Remove the magazine and cycle the weapon to be sure it's empty; push in the recoil spring at the front of the barrel bushing, rotate the bushing to the right, and remove it (allow the recoil spring to come part way out); push out the slide release lever from right to left of the receiver; push the slide forward off the frame; carefully push the recoil spring and rod toward the front of the slide to release and lift the spring and rod out; remove the barrel; lift out the hammer/sear assembly from the receiver. Further disassembly is not normally required, but the stocks can be released by rotating their metal locking lugs inside the magazine well, the firing pin can be removed by pushing the retaining pin from the right side of the slide, and the hammer can be removed by punching out its three retaining pins. The trigger and its spring can be removed by driving out the magazine release catch from the right

side of the frame. Reassembly is a reversal of these procedures.

Specifications

Overall length: 7.68 inches
Weight (unloaded): 1.88 lbs.
Barrel length: 4.57 inches
Magazine capacity: 8

TZ-75/TA-90

The TZ-75 and TA-90 are identical pistols imported into the U.S. by different companies. The TZ-75 is imported by F.I.E. and the TA-90 by Excam. The pistol—with either name—is an Italian copy of the Czech CZ 75, and is made by Fratelli Tanfoglio SPA of Brescia.

Unfortunately, the safety was moved from the frame to the slide and a hammer-drop mechanism added. While this makes sense from a safety standpoint, it created a very awkward system. While it is possible to carry the weapon with the safety off and hammer down, the lack of an internal trigger-coupled firing-pin block makes this unsafe.

The first models imported into the U.S. in late 1982 had an especially awkward safety which had to be turned almost 180 degrees to go from safe to fire. Newer models have a shorter stroke and are more easily engaged with the thumb. The slide release has also been extended and moved toward the grip for easier manipulation. New models with these two improvements are designated either the TZ-75B or TA-90B. A chromed version of the pistol, the TZ-75C, is also available.

Tanfoglio has recently produced a chopped version which holds 12 rounds and is shorter overall. The pistol is currently imported by Excam and is referred to as the "Baby TA-90." The "Baby" has a 4-inch barrel.

The rear sight on all models is adjusted by drifting. It has white inserts to make it easier to see. The front sight has a vertical white line down it; this makes it easy to misalign when firing at a light-colored target. Owners might consider darkening the front sight.

The real plus of the TZ-75 and TA-90 is their price; it is very competitive with others on the market. The pistols can be modified to be carried cocked and locked by a gunsmith which, coupled with the slightly less awkward new safeties, makes them a pretty good combat weapon, though not as good as the Browning Hi-Power. The TZ-75/TA-90s also are not nearly as safe as pistols with internal trigger-coupled safeties.

To field-strip, remove the magazine and cycle the action to be sure it is empty; pull the slide back until the proof marks on the slide rail and frame are lined up; push out the slide release lever from right to left of the receiver; release the slide and allow it to run forward off the frame; carefully push the recoil spring and rod toward the front of the slide to release and lift the spring and rod out; finally, remove the barrel. Reassembly is a reversal of this procedure.

Specifications are nearly identical to that of the CZ-75.

WALTHER P-38

The P-38 was created following the Nazi takeover of Germany. The weapon was designed by Fritz Walther with development beginning around 1935. One of the first models was the AP *(Armee Pistole)*, which had an internal hammer. This design was altered after testing to become the HP *(Heeres Pistole* or Service Pistol) and was marketed in 1937. The German Army adopted it in 1938 as the P-38. A year later the Swedish Army also adopted the Walther as the P-39 but only a few of these were delivered before World War II broke out.

With the war, increased demand for the pistols outstripped the Walther plant's capacity, so production was also carried out at the Mauserwerke and Spreewerke GmbH. Many of these wartime pistols are very crudely finished, and were occasionally sabotaged. Therefore, care should be taken before firing any World War II vintage P-38s.

The P-38 locks up with a tipping block system that is now used in several modern pistols. The trigger/hammer mechanism is basically a scaled-up PP design and includes the double-action trigger and hammer-drop safety. The P-38's internal safety is placed farther forward, however, so that it blocks the firing pin rather than the hammer until the trigger is pulled. The somewhat awkward slide safety acts as a hammer drop and also blocks the hammer from the firing pin when the safety is engaged. Because of the stress created on the safety when the hammer hits it, it is recommended that the hammer be held by the thumb and eased down when engaging the slide safety of any wartime pistol.

The P-38 has dual recoil springs, which allow for a very short slide and receiver. Care should be taken during takedown: the springs can fly out at a dangerous velocity.

A wide variation of models of the P-38 has been produced. Following World War II, the P-38 was manufactured in Walther's new plant in Ulm in 1957 and later in the Manurhin plant in France in 1968. These new models are often designated P-1, since the pistol was adopted as the West German Army's P1, or as the (Swedish) Pistol m/39 as well as P-38; these pistols have aluminum frames. Several versions are currently available which are identical except for barrel lengths; the standard P-38 has a 5-inch barrel, the P4 has a 4.5-inch barrel, and the P-38K has a 2.75-inch barrel.

The P-38 has proven to be very reliable and often quite accurate. The only shortcomings are its somewhat awkward thumb safety, a double-action-only first shot, and a limited magazine capacity.

Specifications

Overall length: 8.38 inches

Weight (unloaded): 2.13 lbs.
Barrel length: 5 inches
Barrel twist: 6 grooves, right-hand
Magazine capacity: 8

WALTHER P5

The Walther P5 was developed after the Palestinian terrorist attack during the 1972 Olympics. It is built around the basic P-38 design. The pistol uses a unique system to keep the firing pin in a safe position until the trigger is pulled: a hole is cut in the face of the hammer which fits the firing pin; when the double-action trigger is pulled, it cams the firing pin upward so that it can be struck by the hammer.

What appears to be a slide release on the left side of the pistol is actually the hammer drop which moves the firing pin into its safe position. Unfortunately, this weapon still uses a magazine release mounted on the base of the pistol grip and the magazine holds only eight rounds. While this conforms to West German needs, it makes the P5 less than ideal for combat. The pistol was adopted by many West German police agencies as well as the Netherlands police.

Field-stripping is quite simple. Remove the magazine and cycle the pistol to be sure it's empty; push the slide back a fraction of an inch; rotate the disassembly lever in front of the left side of the trigger guard downward; pull the slide forward off the frame; and depress the locking plunger and remove the barrel. Reassembly is a reversal of this procedure (be sure the locking block is pushed up above the frame).

Specifications

Overall length: 7 inches
Weight (unloaded): 1.78 lbs.
Barrel length: 3.54 inches
Magazine capacity: 8

WALTHER P-88

The Walther P-88 was introduced in 1983 and entered into the U.S. JSSAP trials. Like other pistols submitted to these trials, the Walther has an ambidextrous safety, double-action trigger, and large-capacity (15 rounds) magazine. The pistol has no external safety and uses a classic Browning lock-up.

The recoil spring is located under the barrel and the hammer is the round, burr style. The rear sights are adjustable for windage. The frame is alloy and the slide steel. The Walther P-88 has a rather different two-function ambidextrous slide release/hammer drop system consisting of a lever on each side of the frame at the front top of the grip plate. Likewise, a magazine release button is located on each side of the pistol just behind the trigger guard.

Field-stripping is simple: remove the magazine and cycle the slide to be sure the weapon is empty; rotate the disassembly lever on the left side of the frame just above the trigger down; push the slide assembly off the front of the frame; remove the recoil spring and guide from the slide; finally, remove the barrel. Reassembly is a reversal of this procedure.

Specifications

Overall length: 7.17 inches
Weight (unloaded): 1.92 lbs.
Barrel length: 4.05 inches
Magazine capacity: 15

.45 ACP Pistols

The vast majority of today's .45 ACP pistols are descendants, if not outright copies, of Browning's old 1911-A1 design. There is nothing wrong with this; the Browning design has proven quite reliable. It can be especially good news when a shooter needs spare parts, since many parts and accessories for the old military pistol can be adapted to the new lookalikes.

There is bad news as well, however. One gun designer confided to me that he and several other manufacturers felt that making a 1911-A1 style pistol without a firing-pin safety that can be engaged when the pistol is being loaded was too risky in these days of product liability.

The old-style inertial firing pin which Browning designed uses a short length and a spring to keep the firing pin from contacting the primer of the cartridge unless hit from the rear by the hammer. That's the theory. In practice, the pistols will sometimes fire if dropped with the hammer down or, more rarely, muzzle first with the hammer back. The 1911-A1 safety locks into the slide and

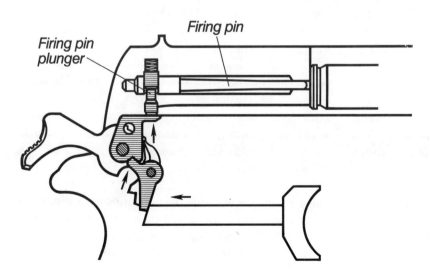

Firing pin plunger

Firing pin

Because the Browning-designed firing pin of the 1911-A1 pistols is considered a bit unsafe by today's standards, many manufacturers are adding a firing-pin block to their pistols. Shown here is the system developed by Colt to lock the firing pin in place with a plunger coupled to the trigger. This system has been incorporated into their Series 80 pistols. Photo courtesy of Colt Firearms.

Pachmayr has a huge selection of accessories for the 1911-A1. Perhaps the most useful are the recoil-eating rubber grips and the extended or ambidextrous safeties, and extended slide releases. Here's a full package of Pachmayr modifications placed on a 1911-A1. Photo courtesy of Pachmayr.

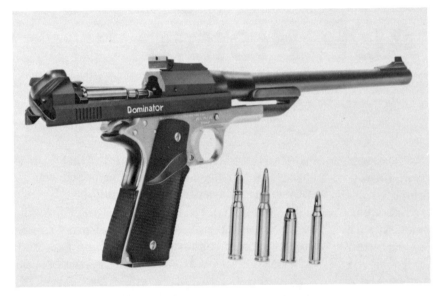

One of the most interesting accessories for the 1911-A1-style pistols is Pachmayr's "Dominator," a bolt-action unit which mounts on the frame of the 1911-A1. The unit quickly converts the pistol into an accurate stockless, single-shot rifle (chambered for .44 Magnum, 7mm BR Remington, .223 Remington, or even .308 Winchester). Photo courtesy of Pachmayr.

must be placed in the fire position in order to cycle a round into the chamber. That places the hammer back with a round in the chamber (and probably the grip safety in fire position as well) until the manual safety can be placed back in the safe position. During this time, accidents are free to happen. Should a shooter try to lower the hammer, it must be done with all safeties, grip and manual, off. Again, an accident waiting to happen.

Colt has done away with some of these problems by creating a firing-pin block coupled to the manual safety. Other pistol designs, like Arminex Trifire, move the safety to the slide where it can be left in the safe position during the loading and while the hammer is lowered. Both solutions make these new pistols a lot safer than the 1911-A1.

A lot of accessories for the 1911-A1 will work well on spinoff pistols. These accessories include the recoil-eating rubber grips offered by Pachmayr and other companies, extended or ambidextrous safeties, extended slide releases, etc. One interesting accessory for 1911-A1 style pistols is Pachmayr's "Dominator," a bolt-action unit which mounts on the frame. The unit quickly converts the pistol into a stockless, bolt-action, single-shot rifle, chambered for .44 Magnum, 7mm BR Remington, .223 Remington, or even .308 Winchester, which can also be scoped. These units are quite accurate; Pachmayr guarantees that the conversion kit will shoot at least one-inch groups at 50 yards. The unit replaces the top slide of standard 1911-A1 type pistols (not the short framed models or the new 80-series Colts without modification, however) and allows the pistol to be converted back to its .45 ACP configuration in just a couple of minutes. Such a unit, costing only around $340, could make a sniper out of a soldier or policeman equipped with a 1911-A1 automatic! It will be interesting to see if the Pachmayr "Dominator" kits go beyond handgun hunter use.

Another accessory is the pistol scope. Unfortunately, unlike a rifle scope, a scope on a pistol is not too quick to use without extensive practice. The scope also needs a custom holster and scopes themselves are relatively fragile. All in all, a scope is not a great aid in combat. However, if you do wish to try such a system, probably the simplest mount is marketed by B-Square. The mount is anchored to the 1911-A1 style pistol's frame (through the slide stop hole) and allows the use of either pistol scopes or the new "red dot" electric scopes.

While the .45 ACP cartridge itself has been made all but obsolete by military forces switching to the 9mm Luger, it still has a large following. Certainly one could do worse than carry a .45 ACP auto for self-defense.

AMT .45 HARDBALLER

The AMT Hardballer pistols are variants of the 1911-A1 Browning automatic, except that the AMT has the 1911-style flat main spring housing. The big difference between the two versions, however, is that the AMT has an extra long slide and 7-inch barrel. This adds some bullet velocity and tames recoil somewhat but creates a weapon that is harder to conceal and handle.

Unfortunately, many early Hardballers were sold with rather rough machined edges, didn't function well out of the box, and often needed tuning before they would fire more than three or four shots without jamming.

If you buy an AMT for combat, be prepared to have a gunsmith do some polishing and adjusting so that it will work properly. And remember that any savings up front can quickly be offset by such hand labor. Takedown is identical to the 1911-A1.

Specifications

Overall length: 10.5 inches
Barrel length: 7 inches
Barrel twist: 6 grooves, left-hand
Magazine capacity: 7

ARMINEX TRIFIRE

The Trifire is a greatly modified 1911-A1 design single-action pistol chambered for .45 ACP, .38 Super, or 9mm Luger. The pistol was designed in 1981 by Jim Mongello to change caliber quickly with suitable kits of barrel, extractor, ejector, and magazine.

The most noticeable change from the Colt design is the lack of a grip safety and the repositioning of the thumb safety from the frame to the slide. Smooth walnut grips extend up the side of the pistol to the lower edge of the slide to give the Trifire a very un-Colt look. The slide has a rib running down its top and the purchaser has a choice of fixed or adjustable rear sights. Another change is the Hi-Power style spring-powered extractor and a spring-loaded ejector rather than the steel bar extractor and ejector normally found on the 1911-A1.

The first Trifires had a hooked trigger guard but the company has plans to switch back to a rounded guard and modify the front and rear sights and internal parts to make the new models stronger. The trigger is made of beryllium copper, giving it a distinctive gold color.

Frame safeties are often awkward to use, but the Arminex safety is an exception to this rule. The Trifire safety is easily snapped into fire position and nearly as easily to safe, where it blocks the firing pin from the hammer and also locks the pin in place. The ability to carry the weapon cocked and locked and to lower the ring hammer with the safety on makes the thumb safety design safer and as easy to use as that of the 1911-A1. While its small magazine capacity might not make it first choice in its 9mm or .38 Super forms, this is one of the first choices for a .45 ACP combat pistol and would be especially useful to own with its conversion kits.

In addition to the standard pistol, ambidextrous safety and long slide target models are also available. The Arminex Trifire is becoming known for its accuracy and dependability. For combat purposes, a throating job may be necessary so the pistol reliably chambers expanding bullets with odd nose shapes.

Field-stripping of the Trifire is slightly simpler than that of the 1911-A1: remove the magazine and cycle the slide to be sure the weapon is empty; pull the slide back to its small takedown notch on the lower rail on the left side of the slide; push the

Arminex Trifire pistols are actually an updated version of the 1911-A1. Note the improved extractor, slightly higher grip, and new alloy trigger. New Trifires will have slightly different sights and a rounded trigger guard. In addition to .45 ACP, kits are available to allow shooters to use 9mm Luger or .38 Super with their pistols. The Trifire is one of the first choices for a combat pistol in .45 ACP. Photo courtesy of Arminex.

Despite the fact that frame safeties are often awkward to use, the Arminex Trifire safety is an exception to this rule. The safety is easily snapped into fire position and nearly as easily to safe where it blocks the firing pin from the hammer and also locks the pin in place. With the ability to carry the weapon "cocked and locked" as well as the ability to lower the ring hammer with the safety on, the pistol is much safer than the 1911-A1. Photo courtesy of Arminex.

slide release lever from right to left of the receiver; push the slide forward off the frame; rotate the barrel bushing; carefully push the recoil spring and rod forward out of the front of the slide; finally, remove the barrel. Reassembly is the reverse of this procedure. Before moving the slide back to the takedown notch, line up the barrel link hole with the frame hole and partially insert the slide release lever, then push the slide on back to the takedown notch and fully insert the lever.

Specifications

Overall length: 8 inches
Weight (unloaded): 2.38 lbs.
Barrel length: 5 inches
Magazine capacity: 7 (9 in 9mm and .38 Super)

ASTRA A-80

The .45 ACP version of the Astra A-80 is nearly identical to the 9mm Luger and .38 Super versions except that its magazine holds 9 rounds rather than 15. (For a fuller description of the A-80, see the 9mm Luger/.38 Super chapter.)

AUTO ORDNANCE .45

Auto Ordnance is the company that since the 1920s has made the Thompson submachine gun. During the late 1950s Auto Ordnance was purchased by Numrich Arms and moved to West Hurley, NY. Since Numrich deals with surplus military parts (including those of the 1911-A1), Auto Ordnance tooled up to produce the pistols in the early 1980s.

The Auto Ordnance pistols are identical to the military models and are made in 9mm as well as .45 ACP. The pistols are made by modern investment casting, which, coupled with their dull military finish, makes them very competitive in price.

The Auto Ordnance pistols can often stand a little smoothing up and perhaps even a trigger job to help improve accuracy. They represent a good buy and are often a better choice than a military surplus pistol of equal price.

BROWNING (COLT) 1911

Following the decision of the U.S. military to go with a .45-size bullet in their handguns, John Browning created the 1905 pistol. While Colt waited for the military's decision on the 1905 gun, the company also marketed it to the public with large sales.

After several delays, the military started tests of .45 revolvers and automatics early in 1907. Savage and Colt came out on top in the tests and the pistols were reworked with 200 of each resubmitted for field testing.

Savage had a terrible time producing the pistols; Colt didn't since it had been turning out its model for some time. After adding a grip safety, loaded chamber indicator, and a few other modifications (including a cut for mounting the always needed—to the turn-of-the-century mind—detachable stock), the 200 Colt pistols were quickly turned out and submitted to the military.

During these tests, the Colt pistols failed in many areas. While part of the problem was poor heat treatment, the major problem was one of design. After addressing these problems, the Model

The Auto Ordnance company is known for its "Thompson" submachine guns. They also market a 1911-A1 pistol which is nearly identical to the military 1911-A1 pistol. While this pistol needs a little throating work for reliability, it is a good buy for those who need a 1911-A1 pistol for self-defense and are willing to get a little work done on it. Photo courtesy of Auto Ordnance Corp.

1909 was developed.

Browning's 1909 pistol resembles the final 1911 pistol. The most important changes on the new pistol were a magazine release behind the trigger guard, alteration of the grip safety, addition of a half-cock notch to the trigger, changing the ejection angle, and a single link-locking system.

The next step was the Model 1910. The cavalry was not happy with the pistol because it could not be carried safely in one hand on horseback, so a final modification was made: an external thumb safety.

The improved Colt 1910 and a modified Savage pistol were tested at Springfield Armory in 1910. The test consisted of firing 6,000 rounds through each pistol. At the end of the test, the Colt had required four replacement parts and the Savage thirteen. Both pistols underwent more changes. The Colt's barrel was beefed up, the manual safety plate enlarged and the left grip plate extended to cover the safety spring/hold open plunger spring, along with a number of other minor changes. Another test took place and the Colt had only minor problems while the Savage had 31 malfunctions and broke a number of parts. Nine days after the report hit the Secretary of War's desk, the Browning became the official Model 1911.

The 1911 pistol proved to be a valuable weapon in World War I, especially in trench warfare. Benedict Crowell, the Assistant Secretary of War, commented:

> Only a few men of each infantry regiment carried pistols when our troops first went into the trenches. But in almost the first skirmish, this weapon proved its superior usefulness in trench fighting.
>
> By midsummer 1917, the decision had been made to supply to the infantry a much more extensive equipment of automatic pistols than had previously been prescribed by the regulations—to build them by the hundreds of thousands where we had been turning them out by thousands.

In 1923, a number of changes were made in the 1911. These were incorporated into newly manufactured pistols and the model redesignated the 1911-A1. The changes consisted of lengthening the hammer, making an arched spring housing at the back of the pistol grip, increasing the length of the spur on the grip safety, shortening the trigger, thickening the front sight, and adding relief cuts to the area around the trigger.

The parts changed on the 1911-A1 were to be interchangeable between the two models so that old pistols might be retrofitted, but in 1932 it was discovered that the Army's engineering drawings were not correct so that Colt parts were not interchangeable with those made in the other plants. This was corrected, but the differences between parts have created headaches for gunsmiths and armorers ever since.

Colt marketed a Super .38 Model of the 1911 in 1929. A large number of its parts are interchangeable with the standard .45 models and it looks nearly identical. In 1935 a Super Match version was made for target shooting; this model is relatively rare, with only 5,000 known to have been made.

In 1931, a .22 LR training version was created as the Ace. It used the same frame and lower parts with a modified slide and barrel. The service model of the Ace used a "floating chamber," so that the .22 LR recoil was amplified to simulate a .45 cartridge. Production stopped during World War II, then resumed after the war. Kits were also offered to convert standard 1911/1911-A1s to the Ace configuration and a rarer kit was also marketed to convert the Ace to .45 ACP.

With the outbreak of World War II, a number of companies manufactured 1911-A1s for the military to meet increased demand. These included Colt, Ithaca Gun Company, Remington Rand, Singer Manufacturing, and the Union Switch and Signal Company. During the first few years of production, the pistols had very poor parts interchangeability. This was corrected in 1943 but, coupled with the error in the engineering drawings which was discovered in 1932, a huge number of pistols was being used which became the bane of repairmen. These problems make assembling a do-it-yourself 1911-A1 pistol from surplus parts an iffy proposition.

During World Wars I and II, Colt and other companies produced 2,337,000 1911/1911-A1 pistols for the government. In addition, it is believed that Colt produced 2,695,000 pistols for commercial sale between the wars. Limited numbers of a small .32 ACP pistol modeled after the 1911-A1 were also made during World War II as the "General Officers Model" for use by high-ranking officers.

In 1949 the U.S. military was thinking about switching to a lightweight 9mm Luger pistol. In an effort to combat such a change, Colt created a model of the 1911 which used an aluminum alloy frame. Coupled with the 3/4-inch shorter barrel/slide, the pistol was 14 ounces lighter than the 1911-A1. Although the military finally decided to stick with the 1911-A1, especially after looking at the cost of replacing all its pistols, Colt marketed its new pistol for civilian sales as the Commander. While this weapon is light, many feel the recoil is excessive and the aluminum frame often doesn't hold up well in extended use. Models of this pistol are chambered for 9mm Luger, .38 Super, and .45 ACP.

Colt continued to manufacture the 1911-A1 for military and civilian sales. In 1957 the Gold Cup pistol was added to the line to capture the target-shooting market. Chambered for either the .38 Super or .45 ACP, these pistols are hand-fitted and have a tight bushing around the barrel and special adjustable sights. While ideal for target shooting, they are not reliable in combat due to their tendency to jam when dirty.

In 1971, the Combat Commander replaced the Commander. Using a steel frame, the weapon was constructed to keep weight to a minimum. Like the Commander, the Combat Commander has a ringed, spurless hammer. In the 1970s, Colt added a collet with fingers to its pistols. This type of collet increases accuracy, but the fingers have a tendency to break under heavy use.

During the 1980s, the safeties of commercial Colt automatics were modified to lock the firing pin when engaged. All older models lock only the sear so that, in theory, the hammer can come loose and fire the weapon or the firing pin *might* have enough momentum to fire a cartridge if the pistol is dropped from a great height. Pistols with this modification are known as the Series 80.

MK IV Series 80 Commander

The new Colt "Series 80 Commander" has a shorter slide and barrel but keeps the standard-size grip. Photo courtesy of Colt Firearms.

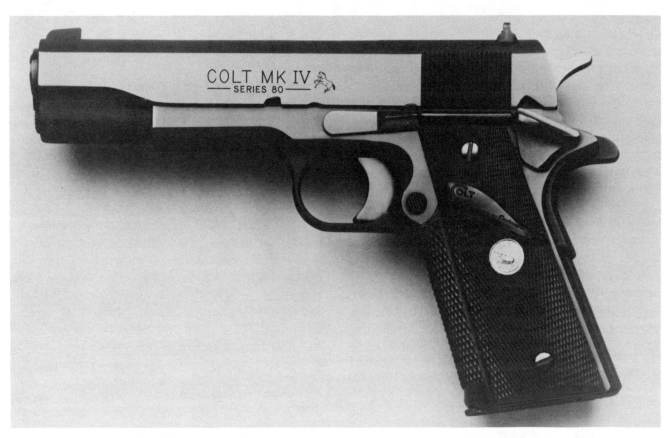

During the 1980s the safety of the standard "MK IV" automatic was modified to lock the firing pin when the safety was engaged. Pistols with this modification to the safety are known as the "Series 80" automatics and are much safer to carry and use than other 1911-A1-style pistols. Photo courtesy of Colt Firearms.

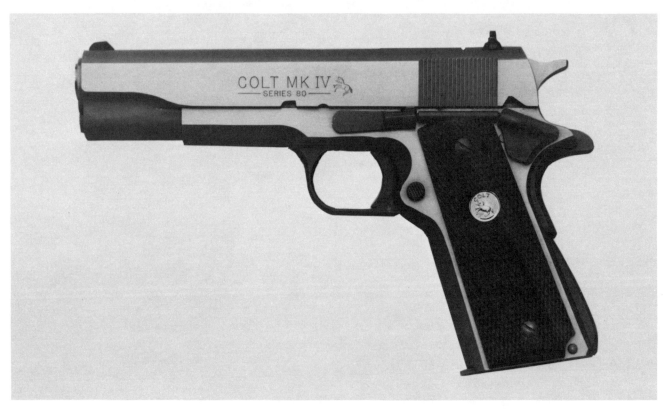

Colt's Series 80 MK IV in stainless-steel is highly durable and offers all the features of the standard blued Colt automatic. Photo courtesy of Colt Firearms.

In 1985, Colt added the stainless steel Government Model, MK IV, Series 80 to its commercial lineup along with a chopped pistol, the Series 80 Officers ACP with both a standard and nickel finish; this pistol has a shortened barrel/slide and grip and the Commander-style ring hammer. Also added was a Lightweight Commander with an aluminum alloy frame.

Colt added the "Series 80 Officers ACP" with nickel finish in 1985; this chopped pistol has both the barrel/slide and grip shortened and sports the burr-style ring hammer similar to that of the Commander. Photo courtesy of Colt Firearms.

Colt's Series 80 Officers ACP with standard blued finish; this chopped pistol makes an ideal hideout pistol for those who want the power of the .45 ACP. Photo courtesy of Colt Firearms.

While Colt had produced a number of improved versions of the 1911-A1, the last U.S. military purchase was in 1945, and those guns were slowly wearing out. The U.S. Air Force was purchasing a number of different automatics and revolvers for air crews. In 1976, the Air Force started its own tests of commercial 9mm automatics and in 1977 the Department of Defense tried to get money for development of a brand new .38-caliber handgun cartridge. A House appropriations committee looking into what was being stocked by the military found that there were 100 different types of ammunition and 25 different handguns in U.S. arsenals, a major supply headache.

The Air Force tests proved inconclusive and the other branches of the military wanted some say in things, so the Department of Defense set up the Joint Services Small Arms Program (JSSAP) in 1978 to find a single cartridge and pistol to be used by all branches. In 1980 the JSSAP recommended that a 9mm Luger handgun be adopted in several versions, one standard-size weapon and a smaller one which could be concealed for special use.

While it was possible to convert 1911-A1s in stock to the Colt 9mm configuration, the guns were so worn that this was deemed unwise. Thus, the race was thrown open to manufacturers to develop a new sidearm. By 1985 a contract had been signed with Beretta to produce the M9 pistol in 9mm Luger.

(Nevertheless, Colt pistols are a favorite of many shooters and a huge supply of surplus parts and aftermarket accessories are available. The Colt 1911-A1 seems to be a gun of legendary proportions. Stories of pistols which function after being caked with mud or that fire tens of thousands of rounds with little visible wear are heard all the time. Many of the stories are probably true.)

A wealth of aftermarket accessories and modifications are available for the 1911-A1 pistol. Probably the most useful are the 8-round magazines which increase the magazine capacity by one (which could be very important in actual combat), and the various types of rubber grips which help the shooter's hold and tame recoil somewhat. Probably the best-known grips are made by Pachmayr in both black and "fashion camo." For those who reload and practice a lot, a rigid brass catcher is available from E&L Manufacturing.

One essential combat modification is to replace any "finger" style barrel bushings on pistols with solid ones. The bushings with small slots cut into

them are slightly more accurate but are also fragile and tend to break. Extended safeties, wide grip safeties, and extended slide releases often are less than ideal in combat. Extended slides are especially prone to locking the slide open or releasing it accidentally during physical movement. Some shooters find larger sights of help, but avoid fragile adjustable sights designed for target shooting. An enlarged ejection port is useful only if you're going to reload your brass; it will normally do little to prevent jams. Occasionally a shooter finds that the flat 1911-style mainspring housing is more comfortable than the A1-style arched hous-

A good magazine is essential for reliable functioning of a 1911-A1. Don't skimp when it's time to buy magazines. Pachmayr offers excellent stainless-steel magazines with a "bumper pad" which aids in getting the magazine seated and helps prevent damage should the magazine be dropped from the pistol during a fast reloading. Photo courtesy of Pachmayr.

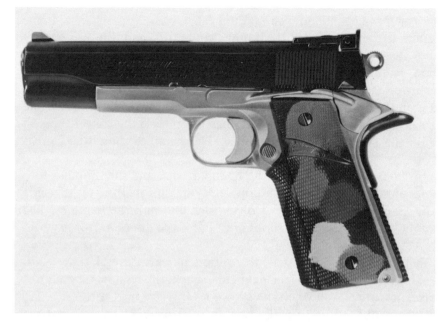

Probably the best known of the rubber custom grips are those made by Pachmayr (available in both black and "fashion camo" as shown). Some shooters maintain that the rubber grips make it hard for a shooter to alter his grip if he draws his weapon with an initially poor hand position, while others feel the Pachmayr grips are all but essential for control and recoil reduction. Photo courtesy of Pachmayr.

ing (Pachmayr offers both styles with a checkered finish); generally the change doesn't make much difference.

Occasionally a "double-action" .45 auto will be encountered. These often have a subassembly that replaces the grip safety and hammer spring housing so that when the pistol is gripped tightly, the hammer is cocked. Other modifications are truly double-action and allow the trigger to lift the hammer for the first shot. Either of these allow the pistol to be carried and still look safe since it isn't cocked and locked. However, such self-cocking arrangements aren't much faster than flipping off the safety of a cocked and locked .45 and take some getting used to. Unless a shooter really needs a double-action 1911-A1, these modifications are best ignored.

Recoil-buffering systems are sometimes helpful to soften up the recoil and save wear and tear on the pistol. Improved accuracy is sometimes claimed with such systems. Just be sure any buffering system is strong; lowered recoil is useless if the unit comes apart.

Several caliber changing kits are available from Colt. One is its .22 LR conversion unit, which is nearly identical to the old Ace adapter kits. A similar kit to allow the conversion of a standard .45 ACP pistol to 9mm is also available though, according to Colt, this kit should be fitted to the pistol by a competent gunsmith.

Magazines can make a good pistol very reliable or unreliable depending on their quality. Avoid no-name surplus magazines and go for quality. In combat, a few dollars saved on cheap magazines could cost you your life.

Many 1911-A1 pistols are made to handle only FMJ ammunition and aren't at all reliable with expanding bullets. A competent gunsmith can cure this by throating the barrel and polishing and widening the feed ramp. Another modification worth considering is having a gunsmith bevel the magazine well slightly so that magazines can be inserted more easily. Encourage him not to remove too much metal, however, as this may weaken the grip enough to fracture easily if dropped. If the trigger pull seems heavy, be sure any work is done by a professional gunsmith; this is not a job for the amateur. (Apparently, General Patton once "tuned" his .45 automatic and had the pistol go off in his holster when stamping about during inspection of the troops. Too much of a good thing makes the 1911-A1 dangerous.)

Some shooters find that the grip safety sometimes prevents them from firing their pistols. Again, a competent gunsmith can defeat the grip safety if that seems necessary.

Don't have the slide tightened or add odds and ends to a combat pistol. Keep it simple. Whatever the modification or accessory, when in doubt, leave it out. Keep modifications to a minimum.

Field-stripping of 1911-A1 and its variants is not hard but is rather complicated. Remove the magazine and pull the slide back to check that the weapon is empty; depress the plug below the muzzle of the barrel; rotate the barrel bushing (which is around the muzzle of the barrel) to the right of the slide to free the recoil plug and spring (on some pistols the bushing is tight and may require a tool to gain enough leverage to do this); and ease the recoil plug out of the front of the slide. Retract the slide until the disassembly cut in its lower edge is lined up with the rear of the slide stop; push the slide stop pivot pin out from the right side of the frame toward the left and remove it from the pistol; allow the slide to run forward off the frame; the recoil spring guide can now be removed from the rear of the slide and the recoil spring, plunger, and barrel bushing from the front of the slide; the barrel can now be removed. Reassembly is the reverse of this procedure.

Though not necessary for normal field-stripping, the firing pin is easily removed by pressing the rear end of the pin, where the hammer strikes it, into the slide and sliding the firing-pin stop up and out of the frame. Take care, as the firing pin is spring-loaded. Once the firing pin and its stop are out, the extractor may be pulled out for repair or replacement.

Because of the number of surplus 1911s on the market, it is good to know how to test the safeties to be sure they are not broken or butchered by a kitchen table gunsmith. After making sure the weapon is empty:

1. Pull back the hammer and place the thumb safety on; grasp the weapon so that the grip safety is depressed and pull the trigger hard; the hammer should not fall.

2. Disengage the thumb safety and remove your hand from the grip safety and pull the trigger; the hammer should not fall.

3. With thumb safety off and the grip safety engaged with your hand, lower the hammer (if the pistol is cocked), then pull the hammer back and— while holding it with your thumb—release the hammer with the trigger so that it is ready to fall. While holding the hammer up, release the trigger then release the hammer. The hammer should be caught by the half-cock notch.

4. With the hammer back and the thumb safety off and the grip safety held properly, pull the slide back 1/16th of an inch and pull the hammer. The hammer should not fall if the disconnector is working properly.

5. Cycle the action quickly several times with the trigger held fully back; the hammer should not fall when the slide goes forward into battery.

6. Finally, dry-fire the pistol to be sure that the pull isn't too light (less than four pounds if you have a gauge). A light trigger pull may mean that the sear is about worn out. A bad sear can cause a pistol either to fire with an unlocked slide or in a full automatic mode!

Even when all the safeties work properly, remember that except for Colt's Series 80 pistols, the 1911-A1 has no firing-pin block and might fire if dropped, even with all the safeties working properly. You should be careful with any pistol and the 1911-A1 and its variants are no exception.

The 1911-A1 and its offspring remain one of the best pistol designs ever developed. The design is tough and reliable. Except for the small magazine capacity, the pistol is an excellent weapon.

Caspian Arms makes its own versions of the 1911-A1. Here are two of their frames, around which the Caspian Arms pistols are built. Note the finger grip and square trigger molded into the lower frame. Caspian frames are made of 4140 steel or stainless steel. Photo courtesy of Caspian Arms.

Specifications

Overall length
(standard Model 1911-A1): 8.5 inches
Weight (unloaded): 2.4 lbs.
Barrel length: 5 inches
Barrel twist: 6 grooves, left-hand
Magazine capacity: 7

CASPIAN ARMS .45

These are basically versions of the Colt 1911-A1. Available on a more or less custom basis, the pistols are made of 4140 steel or stainless steel in the standard configuration or with long slide, short slide, finger-grip frame, etc., according to the buyer's specifications. Caspian Arms also offers the pistols in 9mm and .38 Super.

DETONICS .45 PISTOL

The Detonics pistols are stainless steel custom versions of the 1911-A1 with a straight back strap. While many standard 1911-A1 parts fit the Detonics pistols, some don't—the Detonics guns are really slightly different versions of the 1911-A1 rather than straight copies. The pistols are available in a number of chamberings including .45 ACP, .451 Detonics Magnum (a "wildcat" developed by Detonics), 9mm Luger, and .38 Super.

The pistols have some very useful modifications, including throating/ramp polishing, beveled magazine well, tuned trigger pull, relieved ejection port,

and a barrel centering system which uses a barrel with an enlarged outside dimension at the muzzle and aids the shot-to-shot accuracy of the pistol.

Detonics also offers two conversion kits. One converts 1911-A1 style pistols to .451 Detonics Magnum; the other is a barrel accuracy kit consisting of a heavy barrel and a recoil guide which returns the barrel to the same position after each shot. Also available from Detonics are 8-round magazines, rear sights, and stainless steel extractors and bushings for standard 1911-A1s.

There are currently three versions of the Detonics 1911-style pistols: the Servicemaster (the standard-sized pistol), the Scoremaster (with either 5- or 6-inch barrel), and the Combat Master (a chopped pistol with 3-1/2-inch barrel and 6-round magazine). All three versions are made of stainless steel and available with either a polished or non-glare matte finish. Avoid the polished finish if you're planning on using the pistol for combat. (A few early Detonics were created in blued steel; these are still occasionally encountered in the used gun market.)

Takedown and specifications of the Detonics are nearly identical to the 1911-A1 except as noted above.

HECKLER & KOCH P7

Heckler and Koch were working on a .45 ACP version of their P7. At the time of this writing, despite waning interest in the .45, it appears that the pistol will be marketed in the United States.

The Detonics 1911-style "Servicemaster." Like other Detonics .45 pistols, it is made of stainless steel and available with either a polished finish or a nonglare matte finish. Note the lack of a barrel bushing and standard Pachmayr grips. Photo courtesy of Detonics.

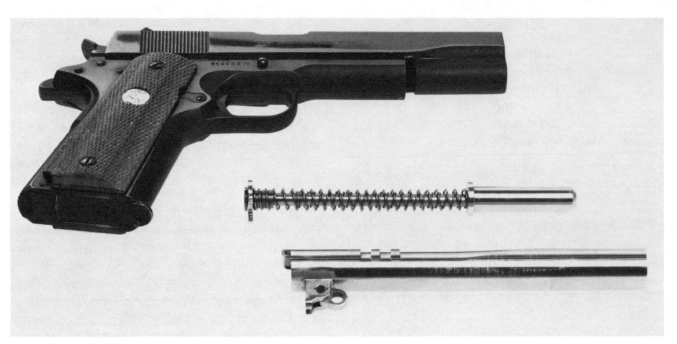

The Detonics System 1 conversion kit is designed for use on various types of 1911-A1-style pistols. The kit consists of a heavy barrel and a recoil guide which returns the barrel to the same position after each shot to improve accuracy. Photo courtesy of Detonics.

The Detonics 1911-style pistol is offered in a "Combat Master" model which is a chopped pistol with 3½-inch barrel and 6-round magazine. Like other Detonics pistols, it is made of stainless steel and is available with either a polished finish or a nonglare matte finish. Photo courtesy of Detonics.

HECKLER & KOCH P9S

The double-action P9S in .45 ACP is nearly identical to the Heckler & Koch 9mm version of the pistol. For more information, see the chapter on 9mm/.38 Super pistols.

The Heckler & Koch P9S is a double-action pistol chambered in .45 ACP. The pistol uses a roller block locking system similar to that used on H&K rifles.

L.A.R. GRIZZLY

The L.A.R. Grizzly is a near-copy of the Colt 1911 but is scaled up somewhat for larger magnum cartridges. Nevertheless, some models of the L.A.R. pistols are chambered for .45 ACP. (For more information, see the following chapter.)

O.D.I. VIKING COMBAT D.A. PISTOL

The Viking pistol is basically a stainless-steel 1911-A1 available in .45 and 9mm. The pistols have the Seecamp double-action modification which allows the first shot to be fired from a hammer-down mode. A short "Combat" model is also available.

RANDALL SERVICE MODEL

Another 1911-style pistol chambered in .45 ACP, 9mm Luger, and .38 Super. Randall also offers a left-handed mirror image version as well as a shortened "Service" model and a chopped-style "Randall Curtis E. LeMay Four Star" model.

SAFARI ARMS .45

These pistols are basically stainless steel 1911-A1s and are usually dolled up for combat competition with adjustable sights, ring hammer, ambidextrous safeties, extended slide release, etc. They are great for contests, but too tight for reliable function. The extended controls often make for inadvertent release/engagement. This pistol is probably best left for target shooting or combat games.

SIG-SAUER P220

The SIG-Sauer P220 is available in a number of chamberings, including .45 ACP. It has a double-action trigger and a firing-pin block which allows for safe carrying of the pistol without a thumb safety or similar device. Early models were cursed with a magazine release on the base of the grip which made it less than ideal for combat; current models feature an ambidextrous thumb-level magazine release which allows for fast magazine changes.

The P220 might be a consideration for someone wanting a .45 automatic similar to a popular 9mm pistol. For more information, see the section on SIG-Sauer pistols in the chapter on 9mm Luger/.38 Super pistols.

SMITH & WESSON 645

The 645 is based on S&W's 39/639 series and works identically to the other S&W automatics. Although S&W was working on a .45 prototype in the 1960s, the pistol wasn't released until 1985; the 645 seems to have come onto the scene a little late, but is a reliable handgun worthy of consideration as a double-action pistol with a hammer drop safety.

The front sight has a red insert, and the rear sight is drift adjustable for windage. The pistol is stainless steel with a satin finish and black checkered nylon stocks. Like other S&W automatics, the 645 has a magazine disconnector safety which can easily be defeated by a competent gunsmith. Unlike many .45s, the S&W 645 can feed a wide variety of bullet nose shapes; many 645s, when new, will even chamber empty brass!

If the 645 proves successful, other models may be introduced (of special interest would be a chopped version similar to the 9mm S&W Model 469). Because the outward dimensions of the 645 are very similar to the 1911-A1, it is a good choice for someone used to the 1911-A1 who

The Smith & Wesson 645 is based on S&W's 39/639 series of semiautos. S&W was working on a .45 prototype in the 1960s, but the pistol wasn't released until 1985. The pistol is a reliable handgun and worthy of consideration for those interested in a double-action pistol with a hammer drop safety. Photo courtesy of Smith & Wesson.

wishes to switch to a double-action pistol.

Takedown is like other Smith & Wesson autos except that the barrel is expanded at the muzzle to do away with the barrel bushing.

Specifications

Overall length: 8.63 inches
Weight (unloaded): 2.34 lbs.
Barrel length: 5 inches
Magazine capacity: 8

SPRINGFIELD ARMORY 1911-A1

The Springfield Armory was a government armory, but has been sold to a private company which has marketed a number of military-style pistols and rifles. Its 1911-A1 pistols are nearly identical to the military versions including the parkerized finish. Because the pistols are combat weapons rather than shiny sporter guns, they are good buys for self-defense.

The weapons are well made and function as well as or better than most military 1911-A1s. Specs are identical to that of the military 1911-A1; a 9mm version is also made.

STAR PD

Spanish pistols patterned after the Browning and Colt designs were first introduced in 1921 by Star Bonifacio Echeverria, S.A., of Eibar. One of the first models, the 1921, had a grip safety but later models have eliminated this feature.

The Springfield Armory is now a private enterprise rather than a government armory. Currently Springfield is marketing its 1911-A1 pistols, which are nearly identical to the military 1911-A1 pistol, including the use of a parkerized finish. Designed for combat, the pistols are good buys for those who need a 1911-A1 pistol for self-defense. Photo courtesy of Springfield Armory.

The early Spanish pistols were chambered for a number of cartridges, including .45 ACP. The Spanish military adopted the Model 1921 as its "Modelo 1922" and Star also marketed the pistol as its Model A. A selective-fire model, the "AD," was also created with the usual detachable shoulder stock which doubled as a holster, but few of these were made.

The Model A/1922 was modified in 1931 and the various models received their own letters, with Model P designating the .45 ACP pistol.

Star currently offers the PD, a chopped, light-weight version of the old P model. The general feeling is that the Star is less reliable than the Colt. Field-stripping is identical to the 1911-A1.

Specifications

Overall length: 7 inches
Weight (unloaded): 1.56 lbs.
Barrel length: 4 inches
Magazine capacity: 6

THOMAS .45

The Thomas .45 was marketed by Alexander James Ordnance, Inc., in Covina, CA, during the mid-1970s. Before the pistol had any success in the marketplace, the inventor died and the factory discontinued production. There are rumors that the pistol will be brought back into production, however, and the first models will probably be in .45 ACP.

The weapon has a Walther PP look to it, though it is larger than the German pistol. It uses a modified blowback system with a grip back strap that moves locking bars up to hold the slide during recoil. At the end of the recoil, the shooter's hand momentarily changes pressure on the grip lock, which then allows the slide to cycle back and load another round. If a loose hold is used which fails to activate the lock, the pistol functions well but recoil is much greater as the slide opens more violently. Because the system allows the barrel to be fixed to the frame, inherent accuracy is potentially much greater.

The trigger is double-action only, with an enclosed striker. Because it uses double-action for each shot, there is no external safety. The only controls are a button magazine release at the rear of the trigger guard on the left grip and a slide release located at the front top edge of the left grip. The pistol uses a short magazine but will accept many 1911-A1 magazines which allow an extra round to be carried.

The sights are fixed, though the rear is drift-adjustable for windage. Finish is believed to have included blue and chrome with a few guns possibly having been made of stainless steel.

The original production pistols work well with Winchester Silvertips. New production pistols, if they become available, should be tested with a variety of ammunition to determine which type works best. Because the weapon works by modified blowback, the full power 230-grain bullets found in many companies' .45 ACP ammunition is not comfortable to shoot, though it will function well.

Takedown is simple: remove the magazine and pull the slide back to be sure the weapon is unloaded; lock the slide open; depress the release levers on each side of the upper rear edge of the frame; pull the slide up and to the rear and off the frame; and remove the recoil spring from around the barrel. Reassembly is a reverse of this procedure.

Specifications

Overall length: 6.25 inches
Weight (unloaded): 2 lbs.
Barrel length: 3.5 inches
Magazine capacity: 6

Magnum Automatics

Shooters by and large have never been enamored with muzzle blast and recoil. Therefore, a magnum cartridge like the .45 Winchester Auto Magnum has a very small following at best. However, all magnums are not created equal; cartridges like the .357 Magnum have little more recoil than 9mm Luger in an automatic action, so the actual recoil of many magnum automatics is considerably less than one might suppose. But what the would-be buyer thinks recoil will be determines whether or not he'll shell out his money; many people who might otherwise own a magnum don't purchase one because they think it will be too hard to handle.

There is also the question of whether the power of a shell like the .45 Winchester Auto Magnum is really needed. It may be interesting to think of a pistol which approaches the energy of a center-fire rifle, but in the real world, such guns often aren't successful if fast followup shots are needed or where overpenetration can be dangerous to bystanders. While the .357 Magnum isn't guilty of much overpenetration with expanding bullets, cartridges like the .45 Winchester Auto Magnum are, especially since they're currently available only

with an FMJ bullet. All in all, it would seem that pistols chambered for cartridges like the .45 Winchester Auto Magnum and 9mm Auto Magnum may be solutions to a nonexistent combat problem. However, the use of multiple-bullet loads might give the magnums the capabilities of burst-fire pistols chambered for smaller cartridges. Three or four flat bullets can easily be nestled in a .357 Magnum or .45 Winchester Auto Magnum cartridge. Each shot would give the equivalent of a 3- or 4-round burst!

The automatic magnum pistols themselves can also be far from ideal. The first strike against them is that they tend to be heavy, both to make recoil manageable and to keep that recoil from quickly destroying the mechanism. This creates a weapon that is uncomfortable to carry and hard to conceal. Magnum pistols also can suffer from poor functioning with the wrong ammunition. If the round is slightly underpowered, the action often won't cycle properly; for this reason, an automatic action also can't enjoy the wide range of load power that a magnum revolver can. While magnum revolver shooters may practice with light loads, most automatic shooters have either to heavily modify their pistol's action to use lighter loads, purchase an adapter kit, or hand-cycle the action—all of which either cost money or are quite inconvenient.

On the plus side, automatics often squeeze more power from cartridges than revolvers, since the blast of the powder is contained in the chamber while part of the gas in a revolver is lost in the cylinder/barrel gap. Another benefit of the automatic is that some of the weapon's recoil is eaten up by the recoil spring. A .357 Magnum fired from a heavy automatic pistol has little more felt recoil than a standard-sized 9mm Luger. The problem of excessive recoil with larger magnum cartridges can also be moderated by about 20 percent with muzzle compensator systems like the "Mag-Na-Port." The trade-off is increased muzzle blast, however. Regardless of porting or lack thereof, ear and eye protection should be used in practice to avoid developing a flinch.

Another trend threatens to displace the magnum automatics from the marketplace. The magnum pistol range is being approached from the other extreme by chopped rifles like the Enforcer, a stockless, short-barreled M1 Carbine, and the Bushmaster, a stockless version of the M16 rifle which uses an ahead-of-the-receiver recoil system and a bullpup pistol grip arrangement. Rifles like these may fill the niche which magnum pistols are trying to occupy. They generally have more power, function as reliably, cost less, and have larger magazine capacity than the magnum automatic pistols. Because the weight of many magnum pistols exceeds three pounds and their size makes them nearly impossible to conceal, many shooters may opt for a lightweight carbine with more power, longer range, more potential accuracy, and larger magazine capacity.

Because of the excessive muzzle blast created by many magnum rounds, muzzle flash can become objectionable at night. Therefore, many shooters might want to try using the new low flash ammunition produced by Federal Cartridge Corporation. The powder in this ammunition is treated to reduce muzzle flash and can be of great help fighting at night.

AUTO MAG

The Auto Mag pistol has been jinxed from the time it was first marketed and seems to change manufacturers with great regularity, manufacturers who shortly go bankrupt.

The pistol was the brainchild of Harry Sanford and its design was carried out by Max Gera in the early 1960s. The pistol was built around a wildcat cartridge based on the .44 Auto Magnum, modified to a rimless configuration by cutting down .380 Winchester cases.

The pistol was marketed in the early 1970s by the Sanford Arms company in Pasadena, CA. By the end of the year, the pistol was to be made by a second company, Auto-Mag Corporation. Anyone who purchased the pistol had to make their own cartridges since they weren't offered commercially. These first pistols had a 6-1/2 inch barrel.

The next year, Auto-Mag went bankrupt and production stopped. The patents, remaining pistols, parts, and machinery were purchased by the Thomas Oil Company which formed a new corporation, TDE. The TDE factory was set up in North Hollywood and Harry Sanford was hired as its chief engineer. In addition to the .45 Auto Magnum chambering, the pistol was offered in 9mm Auto Magnum, another wildcat which later became the 9mm Winchester Auto Magnum.

In 1974 High Standard Corporation took over marketing the pistol while TDE continued its manufacture. A wide variety of pistols was made by TDE, including the standard 6-1/2 inch barrel model. An 8-1/2 inch barrel was also offered without the rib used on the standard barrels and customized pistols were marketed as the Lee Jurras Special. The company also developed a kit to switch from one caliber to the other and offered 5-, 6-, 7-, 8-, and 10-inch barrels.

The market just wasn't there, and the pistol was discontinued in 1975. From there, Harry Sanford set up the AMT corporation which markets the Hardballer .45, Lightning, and Backup, among other pistols. Despite its problems, Winchester was persuaded to manufacture the magnum cartridges designed for the pistol, mainly because the cartridge had become quite popular with target shooters using single-shot pistols like the TC contender.

Part of the problem with the Auto Magnum was shooters' fear of its powerful recoil and the extremely close manufacturing tolerances, which created fitting problems and sensitivity to dirt. Added to this, the gas-operated action creates problems in the form of unburnt powder and added weight.

The Auto Magnum pistols now have happy owners, but most are gun collectors rather than shooters. The pistol has been used to great effect by macho men like Charles Bronson and Clint Eastwood, but has not fared well off the silver screen.

Specifications

Overall length: 11.5 inches
Weight (unloaded): 3.53 lbs.
Barrel length: 6-1/2 inches
Magazine capacity: 7

BREN TEN

The Bren Ten was introduced in 1983 and is more or less the brainchild of Jeff Cooper, the guru of combat shooters. Unfortunately, the pistol is built around a new cartridge. Pistols which require a cartridge not used by any other gun have almost always been slow to gain acceptance and usually quick to leave the marketplace.

The Bren Ten cartridge is sort of a cross between the 9mm Luger and .45 ACP. It splits the caliber size between .45 and 9mm and maintains the velocity of the Luger round while increasing the bullet weight to near .45 proportions. On paper this looks ideal, but the bullet has never been tested in combat, on live animals, or even on ballistic gelatin. Purchasing a Bren Ten is an exercise in faith.

The pistol itself is manufactured by a small company, Dornaus & Dixon Enterprises. The design is based on the CZ 75 pistol with the same size and shape except for changes to accommodate the larger cartridge. Unfortunately, perhaps in an effort to avoid liability suits, a cross bolt firing-pin block was added to the slide which is easily accidentally engaged with potentially disastrous results in combat. Worse yet, this safety is placed high on the slide and is very hard to reach.

The pistol fires from a double-action trigger but can be carried cocked and locked with the safety on. The safety is reversible so an ambidextrous safety is more or less done away with.

The pistol has had some problems. The Bren Tens have been slow to be manufactured despite the fact that large numbers were sold in advance in an aggressive marketing campaign. Hard on the heels of this problem was a shortage of magazines due to problems with a subcontractor. With endless delays before the first pistols could be delivered, Dornaus & Dixon Enterprises was flooded with letters and calls of complaint and pleas for more information. The company was slow to respond and also sent out some less than diplomatic letters which further infuriated many would-be buyers. Therefore, the company has a rather bad image it is going to have to patch up if it is to succeed in selling the Bren Ten. Perhaps the final irony for people who paid for the pistol years before receiving one was that the Bren Ten appeared on the popular TV show *Miami Vice* in the hands of actor Don Johnson.

Those who aren't sold on the Bren Ten cartridge see little advantage in the pistol, although a .45 ACP conversion unit is available to pick up some of the .45 market. The gun is made with what one critic called a "melted look," with the lines being rounded off (apparently when the gun is polished to remove machining marks) by the factory. To those used to the sharp machined lines of most weapons, this look is far from attractive.

The rear sight is adjustable for windage and elevation, and the pistols are made with a stainless steel frame. The barrel comes throated and the feed ramp is polished. Several models are available, including a chopped pocket model. Finishes (which are often two-tone because of the difference in slide and frame steels) include matte black, hard chrome/stainless steel, blued/oxide, and nickel/stainless.

The bottom line is that the Bren Ten has a lot of things going against it even though it may well be a fine pistol chambered for a very effective cartridge. Few know for sure if this is true, and many of those who have gambled on buying one feel like they've been stung. Not a good beginning for a pistol.

The Bren Ten appears to be a good idea that, through poor luck and marketing, may not get off the ground. Disassembly is similar to that of the Hi-Power.

Specifications

Overall length
(standard model): 8.37 inches
Weight (unloaded): 2.45 lbs.
Barrel length: 5 inches
Magazine capacity: 11 (9 in .45 ACP)

COONAN

The Coonan pistol is based on the Browning

1911-A1 with its parts reworked and enlarged to accommodate the .357 Magnum. Design work was done by Dan Coonan during the early 1980s.

The Coonan is made of stainless steel except for the barrel, which is made of a tougher steel capable of resisting the pressures and friction created by the .357 Magnum. The machining tolerances on current models of the Coonan are tight; be sure to put at least five hundred rounds through the gun to lap parts so that they fit each other and for the best reliability. The manufacturer recommends using lithium grease during this period for reliable functioning. Early Coonan pistols used a swinging link to lock the barrel; newer pistols use a Hi-Power-style lug which appears to be more reliable. The older pistols are now classed as the Model A while the newer pistols with the lug rather than a link are the Model B.

One other change from the 1911-A1 is readily noticeable: the use of a pinned, spring-loaded extractor rather than one of spring steel. Another departure from the Browning design is pinning the trigger to the frame, which greatly aids the trigger pull.

In order to make the pistol function reliably during chambering, several design tricks were employed. First, the cartridges feed almost directly into the chamber, minimizing the size of the feed ramp. Second, a projection from the barrel extends over the cartridges during feeding so that they are guided right into the chamber. This creates one problem with the Coonan; the chamber can only be loaded from the magazine and the magazine can be inserted only when the slide is back. This makes some problems and limits the pistol to 7 rounds; you can't add another round to the magazine after loading the chamber. The magazine spring itself is very stiff, but a small hole in the magazine carrier and a long cut down both sides allow a tool to be used to retract the carrier as shells are loaded. (The side cuts in the magazine also allow the number of rounds in the magazine to be quickly determined.)

In order to accustom the shooter to the Coonan's larger size, the slide release and safety are extended. The extended slide release can be a problem if the shooter hits it during recoil; care should be taken to develop a shooting hold which avoids inadvertent engagement. The base of the grip is also beveled to speed up reloading and the hammer is a circular burr shape like the Colt Commander. Because of these design changes,

no 1911-A1 parts are interchangeable with the Coonan.

The front sights are manufactured too high; this is to allow the owner to file them down to zero the pistol to the owner's loads. Great care should be taken in doing this since the metal is hard to put back! The rear sight is adjustable by loosening a set screw. The screw should be checked from time to time to be sure it hasn't shaken loose.

Although the Coonan has a rather short barrel, bullets fired from it still have a higher velocity (by around 100 fps) than a revolver with an eight-inch barrel. Functioning of the pistol with full-powered loads is nearly perfect. Winchester 145-grain Silvertips and similar ammunition work well. Unlike the larger .44 Winchester Auto Magnum, the .357 Magnum doesn't create excessive recoil or muzzle jump; the Coonan is nearly as controllable as most .45 automatics.

An added plus with the Coonan is a .38 conversion kit which allows the use of standard .38 Special rounds. Unlike most major conversions, the conversion to .38 only requires changing the recoil spring and the magazine. A change to a slightly weaker spring will also allow the pistol to function with reduced loads. Takedown is identical to the 1911-A1.

Specifications

Overall length: 8.3 inches
Weight (unloaded): 2.6 lbs.
Barrel length: 5 inches
Magazine capacity: 7

DESERT EAGLE

The Desert Eagle is produced by Israeli Military Industries, apparently only for export to the U.S. and a few other countries. It is available in both .357 Magnum and .44 Magnum with conversion kits allowing the owner to change to the second caliber. The pistol was first released in the U.S. in 1982.

The pistol has a lot of nice features: adjustable sights, an integral scope mount (with a longer detachable mount for larger scopes), adjustable trigger pull (with a single-action-only trigger system), four barrel lengths (6-, 8-, 10-, and 14-inch), and four finishes to choose from (namely, stainless steel, blued steel, satin nickel, and chrome).

The pistols come with neoprene grips that help minimize recoil; both steel and aluminum alloy frames are available.

The controls are set up fairly well, too, with a basic Browning layout except for the slide-mounted ambidextrous safety, which is hard to reach. The Desert Eagle pistol has a reputation for pointing well; most shooters find it easier to shoot accurately with this pistol than with others.

Internally, the pistol is different from most automatics and is, in fact, more like a rifle. It uses a rotating three-lug bolt which is rotated open by the gas action of the cartridge. In theory, the rotating bolt should allow the pistol to function with some leeway for various types of ammunition. In practice, the Desert Eagle seems to be a bit ammo-sensitive. It functions reliably, however, with several brands of 158-grain hollow-point ammunition. Those who plan on using a Desert Eagle for self-defense should experiment to find what brand of ammunition works best. With the wrong ammunition, the pistol tends to malfunction with terrible regularity.

Though the pistol has a few problems, it is entirely possible that these bugs will be exorcised in the near future. Even if no improvements are made, the firearm still holds a lot of promise. About the only drawbacks are the awkward safety and large size.

Field-stripping is easy: remove the magazine and cycle the weapon to be sure it's empty; push in the diassembly button on the left of the frame (over the forward end of the trigger guard); rotate the disassembly lever on the right side of the frame (at the forward end of the trigger guard); lift out the barrel; push the slide off the frame; remove the recoil springs from the frame. Reassembly is basically a reversal of this procedure.

Specifications

Overall length: 10.25 inches
Weight (unloaded): 3.25 lbs.
Barrel length: 6 inches
Magazine capacity: 9

DETONICS .45 PISTOL

The Detonics pistols are stainless steel custom versions of the 1911-A1 with a straight back strap. In addition to the standard .45 ACP chambering, the pistols are offered in .451 Detonics Magnum

(a wildcat developed by Detonics). The user of the .451 cartridge is committed to reloading his own ammunition since it isn't commercially available and, while this cartridge has more power than the standard .45, whether it has a decisive edge over the .45 or 9mm is doubtful. Given the smaller magazine capacity, it would seem better to go with a large-capacity 9mm Luger like the Beretta 92 series or the Browning Hi-Power. For more information, see the .45 ACP chapter.

L.A.R. GRIZZLY

The L.A.R. Manufacturing Company was created in 1968 and currently manufactures machine gun tripods and M-16 receivers for the U.S. government. The company introduced the Grizzly pistol in 1983. The handgun is a near copy of the Colt 1911 but scaled up to accept larger magnum cartridges. All but ten parts of the Grizzly will exchange with those of the Colt 1911-A1. This simplifies manufacturing and also gives the owner a cheap source of parts. For those who wish to shoot magnum cartridges in a 1911-style pistol operation, this would seem an ideal choice.

In addition to the .45 Magnum chambering, conversion kits are also offered by the company to change the chamberings to .45 ACP, .45 Winchester Magnum, and .357 Magnum. The company has announced plans to add the .30 Luger, .30 Mauser, .38 Special Wadcutter, 9mm Luger, 9mm Steyr, 9mm Browning Long, 9x18 Ultra Police, 9x18 Russian Makarov, and 9mm Winchester Magnum! If so, this would create one of the largest kit guns ever made. The conversion kits each consist of a barrel, recoil spring, ejector, extractor, and magazine. This is a multi-cartridge gun if ever there was one. Important: take care not to mix up the parts from different kits or functioning will go down the drain.

With the .45 Magnum (and most other cartridges), the Grizzly functions well with factory ammunition and will function well with carefully tailored reloads. However, for best accuracy, the shooter should experiment to find the best ammunition for the pistol.

The Grizzly pistol comes in two versions. The Mark I comes with a lot of custom features including an adjustable rear sight, beveled magazine well, Pachmayr grips, polished feed ramp, throated barrel, adjustable trigger, and ambidextrous thumb safety. It is also designed with a solid barrel bush-

The "Grizzly" pistol is a near copy of the Colt 1911, but scaled up somewhat so that it will accept larger magnum cartridges. All but ten parts of the Grizzly will exchange with those of the Colt 1911-A1. This is the Mark I version with adjustable rear sight. Photo courtesy of L.A.R. Manufacturing.

Like the Mark I, the Mark II Grizzly (shown) is capable of firing a wide range of ammunition with the proper adapter kits. The Mark II is the low-cost version of the Grizzly and is easily recognized by its nonadjustable rear sight. Photo courtesy of L.A.R. Manufacturing.

ing and has an extended magazine release. The Mark II version lacks the adjustable rear sight.

If you're looking for a magnum automatic, the Grizzly offers the reliability necessary for combat. Takedown is identical to the Colt 1911-A1 and—if the pistol ever needs to be repaired—any gunsmith familiar with the 1911-A1 will be able to work on the Grizzly without problem.

Specifications

Overall length: 10.5 inches
Weight (unloaded): 3.19 lbs.
Barrel length: 6.5 inches
Magazine capacity
(in .45 Winchester Magnum): 7

Appendix I

Ballistic Tables for Common Combat Rounds

Your firearm is only as effective as the ammunition you put in it. While ammunition that allows the weapon to function properly is important, the choice of ammunition goes well beyond this. Modern bullet design can give a fighter an added advantage by increasing a weapon's lethality without increasing its weight and recoil. This is especially true of the new expanding bullets from companies like Winchester, Federal, and CCI.

Some "gimmick" bullets like the Glaser Safety Slug, high-velocity bullets, or multiple-projectile ammunition may also give a fighter an edge in combat (for a full look at this important aspect of combat, see my book *Combat Ammunition,* available from Paladin Press). Care must be taken to be sure such ammunition will function reliably in a pistol. Too, such ammunition may be hard to find unless you're willing to reload the cartridges yourself.

Getting your bullet on target is also a major problem. Practice and proper zeroing of the weapon are essential. Careful study of the ballistic charts below (as well as those in reloading manuals and other sources) will help you get your bullets to the target.

Since the pistol is most often involved in combat at ranges varying from arm's length to seven yards, the need to worry about bullet drop, or even aiming, is often not too great. However, there are cases of pistols being used in combat at ranges in excess of 100 yards. At ranges of 100 yards or more, the bullets from even the lowly .32 ACP and .380 Auto are capable of causing grave injury, and .22s and .25 ACP can be used in harassing fire. Thus, a man armed with a pistol may engage opponents with shotguns or even rifles successfully from such ranges provided he is a very good shot, is aware of bullet drop at such ranges, and is very lucky to boot.

At extreme ranges, or with very short barrels, bullet velocity becomes an important consideration, especially with expanding bullets. Generally, a velocity of 705 to 800 feet per second (fps) is needed for a hollow-point bullet to expand reliably (and expansion won't be as full as it would at maximum speed) and 1,115 fps is needed with a soft-point bullet. Thus the hollow-point bullet gives a longer range/wounding capability than its soft-point counterpart. The firearm's ability to chamber the round is also an important consideration with semiauto firearms; soft points will often feed more reliably than hollow points in older handguns.

Zeroing a handgun for bullet drop at specific range isn't too critical within most distances at which handguns are used. Of course windage is critical; a pistol should shoot dead on target. If a pistol will hit point of aim within 25 yards, it is ready for all but long-range combat use. Such a zero will allow you to fire at normal combat ranges without adjusting your aim for change in point of impact—since that isn't much of a consideration anyway. At extreme ranges of 100 yards or more, you could then guesstimate the bullet drop and raise the front sight well above the rear sight. A lot of practice and awareness of bullet drop at different ranges are the only ways to obtain long-range accuracy.

Bullet velocities will vary greatly from one brand of ammunition to another and from one firearm to another. Barrel length can also make some difference in velocity, though often not as much as one might think. Semiauto pistols often milk a higher velocity from ammunition than revolvers because of the gas leak in the gap between the cylinder and throat of the barrel. Therefore, rounds like the .357 Magnum or .38 Special, when used in automatics, will have a higher muzzle velocity than manuals may specify.

In general, the higher a bullet's velocity, the more damage it will create. New ammunition takes advantage of this fact by using lightweight bullets fired at high velocity. Some exotic new ammunition uses extremely lightweight bullets which approach the cutoff point (2,000 fps) of high-velocity rifle bullets. Because the speed is created by using lightweight bullets, this type of ammunition loses its velocity quickly and is suitable only for close combat.

As you look over the figures below, remember that the actual numbers for your gun and ammunition may vary greatly from those shown, especially if your pistol's barrel is shorter or longer than the average length of similar weapons. These tables should be used for reference only.

Included in the chart are the bullet's foot pounds of energy (fpe) at various ranges. Foot pounds of energy are good for comparing energy levels within a certain caliber but do not tell a lot about wounding capability. Factors such as bullet design and speed come into play, so it is a mistake to assume that one caliber of bullet is more lethal than another simply because it has more foot pounds of energy at a given distance.

Multiple hits striking the target at the same instant are necessary for quick stopping power with FMJ (full metal jacket) bullets in most pistol calibers. When using such diminutive calibers as the .22, .32 ACP, and .380 ACP, the chances of success in combat (except for lucky hits or three-round burst fire) are extremely doubtful. With expanding bullets or multiple-projectile rounds, the .38 Special, 9mm Luger, .38 Super, .357 Magnum, and .45 ACP will generally be adequately effective in combat. In general, a faster bullet which expands will be much more lethal than its heavier counterpart on all but armored targets.

Since 108 foot pounds of energy is considered the minimum needed to create a serious wound (and not an instantly disabling one at that), a little study of the charts will show just how minimal many rounds are, especially at extended ranges.

.22 SHORT

The .22 Short is of dubious use in combat though it might be better than nothing at all. Shots would have to be very well placed to be effective. In a semiauto pistol coupled with a silencer, the .22 Short does have some use among special forces or in covert activities. Shot placement and surprise would be critical for successful use of the .22 Short.

.22 SHORT (29-GRAIN)

	Muzzle	50 yds.	100 yds.
Velocity (fps)	1045	951	872
Energy (fpe)	70	58	49
Deviation (in.)	0	5	29

.22 LONG RIFLE

The .22 rimfire dates back to the Flobert BB Cap of 1845 and the Smith & Wesson .22 Short of 1857. There was once a whole family of rimfire ammunition, including .44 caliber rifle ammunition, but the larger cartridges were unable to contain the pressures created by smokeless powder and thus became obsolete. Only the .22s remain.

Of the .22s now available, probably the .22 Long Rifle is the most useful. Maximum velocity with most .22 Long Rifle ammunition is achieved with a 6-inch barrel. Beyond this length, an actual decrease of velocity will result (along with decreased noise levels). Although it would seem that high-velocity ammunition designed for use in rifles would not be most ideal in pistols, in fact, ammunition like CCI's Stinger and Mini-Mag are probably the most potent .22 Long Rifle ammunition for combat. Because of the differing functioning abilities of .22 semiautos, great care should be taken to test out .22 ammunition with the pistol it is to be used in.

CCI's CB caps may also be of use in some types of covert activities such as quietly dealing with guard dogs or knocking out floodlights or for quiet indoor practice. This ammunition is loaded with a 29-grain bullet over a small charge of powder in a Long Rifle case.

All .22 ammunition seems to be extra sensitive to moisture and oil; take care not to accidentally deactivate the cartridges.

.22 LONG RIFLE (38-GRAIN)
2½-INCH BARREL

	Muzzle	50 yds.	100 yds.
Velocity (fps)	917	701	498
Energy (fpe)	71	41	21
Deviation (in.)	0	2	14

.22 LONG RIFLE HIGH-VELOCITY (32-GRAIN)
2-INCH BARREL

	Muzzle	50 yds.	100 yds.
Velocity (fps)	1146	971	827
Energy (fpe)	93	67	49
Deviation (in.)	0	1	11

.22 LONG RIFLE HIGH-VELOCITY (32-GRAIN)
6-INCH BARREL

	Muzzle	50 yds.	100 yds.
Velocity (fps)	1560	1282	1090
Energy (fpe)	173	117	84
Deviation (in.)	0	1	11

CCI .22 CB MINICAP/MINI-CAP LONG
(29-GRAIN)

	Muzzle	50 yds.	100 yds.
Velocity (fps)	727	667	610
Energy (fpe)	33	28	24
Deviation (in.)	0	1	11

.25 AUTOMATIC (COLT) PISTOL (6.35mm AUTO)

Most .25 ACP ammunition is actually slightly less effective than modern high-velocity .22 Long Rifle rounds. Therefore, this round is generally a second choice for combat use. John Browning developed the .25 ACP in the early 1900s when he encountered difficulties in creating a pistol that could chamber the rather crude .22s of the day. Today, provided bargain basement .22 LR ammunition isn't being used, the .22 is nearly, if not as, reliable as the .25 ACP.

One new brand of ammunition which slightly outperforms the .22 Long Rifle in short-barreled hide-away pistols is the MSC, which uses a 29-grain brass hollow point. This can give the .25 ACP pistol a slight edge over the .22 LR.

.25 ACP/6.35mm MSC (29-GRAIN)
2-INCH BARREL

	Muzzle	50 yds.	100 yds.
Velocity (fps)	1225	997	854
Energy (fpe)	97	64	47
Deviation (in.)	0	−2	−9

.25 ACP/6.35mm (45-GRAIN)
2-INCH BARREL

	Muzzle	50 yds.	100 yds.
Velocity (fps)	850	760	683
Energy (fpe)	72	58	46
Deviation (in.)	0	−1.5	−6.3

.25 ACP/6.35mm (50-GRAIN)
2-INCH BARREL

	Muzzle	50 yds.	100 yds.
Velocity (fps)	760	707	659
Energy (fpe)	64	56	48
Deviation (in.)	0	−2	−8.7

.32 AUTOMATIC/7.65mm BROWNING

The .32 Auto was designed by John Browning for use in one of his automatic pistols which was marketed in 1899. The round was popular due to its low power, which made it usable in relatively inexpensive blowback pistols. Currently, it appears that the .32 Auto is being displaced by the .380 ACP, which outperforms it while accommodating a pistol size as small as that of the .32. The .32 Auto is much better than any .25 ACP or .22 LR cartridge and if the choice is between the .32 or one of these lesser cartridges, the .32 wins hands-down with modern expanding bullets.

.32 AUTO/7.65mm (71-GRAIN)

	Muzzle	50 yds.	100 yds.
Velocity (fps)	905	855	810
Energy (fpe)	129	115	97
Deviation (in.)	0	− 1.4	− 5.8

.32 AUTO/7.65mm (110-GRAIN)

	Muzzle	50 yds.	100 yds.
Velocity (fps)	1295	1094	975
Energy (fpe)	410	292	232
Deviation (in.)	0	− 0.8	− 3.5

.32 AUTO/7.65mm (125-GRAIN)

	Muzzle	50 yds.	100 yds.
Velocity (fps)	1450	1240	1090
Energy (fpe)	583	427	330
Deviation (in.)	0	− 0.6	− 2.8

.380 ACP/9mm BROWNING SHORT

This round was created by John Browning in 1912. Although the .380 ACP is popular among European police units and military bodies, it is considered marginal at best by most modern combat experts.

For combat use, the Glaser Safety Slug is best in this chambering provided it functions well and chambers reliably; the Winchester Silvertip is runner-up ballistically, but functions well in nearly all .380 ACP semiauto pistols.

In theory, the .380 ACP round might be used out to 150 yards, as shown in the chart below.

.380 ACP/9mm BROWNING SHORT (90-Grain)

	Muzzle	50 yds.	100 yds.
Velocity (fps)	955	865	785
Energy (fpe)	190	160	130
Deviation (in.)	0	0	− 11.4

Such hits would cause serious injury but would not be easily delivered even with a 100-yard zero.

Some .380 pistols that use a locking system rather than straight blowback can be rechambered and reworked by a competent gunsmith to fire 9mm Luger. This creates a very potent pistol of small size.

.30 (7.65mm) LUGER

This bottle-necked cartridge was developed with the introduction of the Luger pistol and has proved inferior to its 9mm counterpart. The .30-caliber bullet tends to overpenetrate and create smaller wounds. Though seldom encountered in the United States, the .30 Luger is popular in Europe (especially Italy and Switzerland). It is also often encountered in countries which don't allow military cartridges to be used by their citizens. With expanding bullets, this round would work for combat, but is really second best when compared to the 9mm Luger.

Almost any pistol chambered for 9mm Luger can be converted to .30 by simply changing the barrel and possibly the recoil spring. While this allows the use of two different calibers in one pistol, it makes little sense from a combat standpoint.

7.62mm RUSSIAN TOKAREV

This bottle-necked cartridge was adopted as the official Soviet cartridge in 1930 for their Tokarev pistols. The cartridge is quite similar to the 7.63mm Mauser, and some Mauser ammunition will actually chamber and function in Tokarev pistols.

While not overly good in combat, like the 7.63mm Mauser, the 7.62mm Tokarev is capable of defeating body armor which will stop most other pistol rounds.

7.63mm (.30) MAUSER

The 7.63mm Mauser cartridge was developed by an American, Hugo Borchardt, for use in his pistol. Both the cartridge and pistol were introduced by Ludwig Loewe Company of Germany in 1883. The Borchardt pistol was later reworked to become the Luger pistol.

The Borchardt cartridge was used by Paul Mauser for his Model 1896 pistol and came to be

.380 ACP/9mm BROWNING SHORT (88-GRAIN)

	Muzzle	50 yds.	100 yds.	150 yds.
Velocity (fps)	1000	921	860	752
Energy (fpe)	189	160	140	113
Deviation (in.)	0	+ 4.5	0	− 16

.30 (7.65mm) LUGER (100-GRAIN)

	Muzzle	50 yds.	100 yds.	150 yds.
Velocity (fps)	1200	1042	957	884
Energy (fpe)	298	241	204	173
Deviation (in.)	0	− 10.2	− 27.6	− 53.5

7.62mm TOKAREV (100-GRAIN)

	Muzzle	50 yds.	100 yds.	150 yds.
Velocity (fps)	1400	1211	1077	983
Energy (fpe)	435	326	258	215
Deviation (in.)	0	− 5.3	− 16.5	− 34.5

7.63mm MAUSER (100-GRAIN)

	Muzzle	50 yds.	100 yds.	150 yds.
Velocity (fps)	1400	1211	1077	983
Energy (fpe)	435	326	258	215
Deviation (in.)	0	− 5.3	− 16.5	− 34.5

known as the "7.63mm Mauser," even though it was actually designed by Borchardt.

The bottle-necked cartridge enjoyed a lot of popularity in Spanish and various Mauser pistols at the beginning of the 1900s but has since fallen into disfavor. While it might be of use with a suitable expanding bullet, because no modern combat pistol is now available for it, the 7.63mm Mauser is a combat round without a firearm.

9mm LUGER (PARABELLUM)/ 9x19mm NATO

This is currently the best designed combat pistol cartridge. It is a good compromise between size and power, and is effective without excessive blast and recoil. The 9mm Luger was introduced with the Luger pistol in 1902. Early cartridges suffered from ineffective bullets; new bullet designs and powders give this round a lot of power. The best may be yet to come. Experimental ammunition being developed in Europe by Norma, for example, can penetrate an American steel hel-

met out to beyond 200 meters.

Because of improvements in this round's performance and the cartridge's adoption as NATO standard, the 9mm Luger is gaining more and more acceptance in the United States and seems to be destined to be the "standard" combat round for semiauto pistols of the near future.

Velocity changes created by barrel lengths in the 9mm Luger are generally in the order of 30 fps per inch of barrel. Consequently, barrel length is a small consideration except, perhaps, for extremely short or long barrels. Velocities shown below are for standard ammunition with a 4-inch barrel.

The Winchester Silvertip is probably the best readily-available 9mm commercial round available; CCI's Blazer and Lawman brand hollow-points are also quite good. The U.S. military is considering adopting a solid-point Blazer as its standard 9mm round, while in law-enforcement circles, Federal hollow-points are widely considered the first choice.

Recently, high-velocity "+P" rounds have been

created for the 9mm. These should be used with caution, as they create quite high chamber pressures. In general, the gain in velocity is probably not worth the extra wear and tear created on the pistol.

.38 COLT SUPER AUTOMATIC

The .38 Super, introduced in 1929, is an improved version of the older .38 Auto. While the .38 Super has not caught on in the U.S. or Europe, it is quite popular in Canada, Mexico, and some South American countries. Most pistols chambered for 9mm Luger can be converted to .38 Super by a competent gunsmith.

.357 MAGNUM

Winchester and Smith & Wesson designed the .357 Magnum in 1935. The cartridge is based on the .38 Special, with the brass lengthened by 1/10th inch to prevent the .357 from being chambered in a .38 Special weapon. While designed for revolvers, the rimmed .357 Magnum can be an ideal round in an automatic, since its recoil is tamed and the bullet velocity improved. In combat, when a large number of shots won't be fired, it is ideal.

With comparable .357 Magnum pistols, there will be from 20 to 60 fps velocity difference for each two inches of barrel length. Semiauto pistols using the .357 Magnum will enjoy higher velocity than revolvers with the same barrel length.

.45 ACP

The .45 ACP was developed by John Browning in 1905 and adopted by the U.S. military, along with Browning's pistol. Recent studies of actual shootings as well as ballistic gelatin and animal tests have shown that the .45 ACP is not the end-all that many of us thought. The .45 is not flat-shooting for long-range engagements, nor is it as good as the 9mm Luger at penetrating modern body armor. There are a lot of good pistols chambered for the .45 ACP, however, and it is certainly better than most semiauto rounds. For best performance, the bullet weight should be light and its nose designed to expand.

.45 WINCHESTER AUTO MAGNUM

The .45 Auto Mag was introduced by Winchester in 1979. The cartridge is more or less a rimless version of the .44 Magnum. While the semiauto action reduces some of the recoil of this size round, the .45 Auto Mag tends to burn dirty. Fouling thus becomes a problem, and functioning may be quite unreliable after extensive shooting with a gas-action system.

While it might be quite effective in combat, the cartridge's size limits the number of rounds a firearm chambered for it can carry. The recoil dictates that a heavy weapon be used, making for a large pistol with a small magazine capacity. Like the .44 Magnum, the .45 Winchester Magnum is probably better suited to hunting than combat. With a lighter bullet, this round would be capable of rifle-like performance and wounding ability.

9mm LUGER (90-GRAIN)				
	Muzzle	50 yds.	100 yds.	150 yds.
Velocity (fps)	1300	1119	1006	928
Energy (fpe)	338	250	202	172
Deviation (in.)	0	+3.05	0	−11.6
Deviation (25-yd. zero)	0	−0.7	−7.52	−22.9

9mm LUGER (115-GRAIN)				
	Muzzle	50 yds.	100 yds.	150 yds.
Velocity (fps)	1155	1047	971	939
Energy (fpe)	341	280	241	225
Deviation (in.; 100-yd. zero)	0	+3.27	0	−11.8
Deviation (25-yd. zero)	0	−0.9	−6.5	−21.5

.38 SUPER (125-GRAIN)
6-INCH BARREL

	Muzzle	50 yds.	100 yds.	150 yds.
Velocity (fps)	1200	1089	1011	957
Energy (fpe)	400	329	284	254
Deviation (in.; 100-yd. zero)	0	+ 3.3	0	− 11.7
Deviation (25-yd. zero)	0	− 0.9	− 8.3	− 24.1

.357 MAGNUM (125-GRAIN)
4-INCH BARREL

	Muzzle	50 yds.	100 yds.	150 yds.
Velocity (fps)	1400	1192	1083	1007
Energy (fpe)	544	394	326	281
Deviation (in.; 100-yd. zero)	0	+ 2.6	0	− 10
Deviation (25-yd. zero)	0	− 0.5	− 6.3	− 19.4

.357 MAGNUM (158-GRAIN)
4-INCH BARREL

	Muzzle	50 yds.	100 yds.	150 yds.
Velocity (fps)	1100	1025	968	920
Energy (fpe)	424	369	328	297
Deviation (in.; 100-yd. zero)	0	+ 3.7	0	− 13
Deviation (25-yd. zero)	0	− 1.1	− 9.7	− 27.6

.45 AUTO (185-GRAIN)

	Muzzle	50 yds.	100 yds.	150 yds.
Velocity (fps)	900	851	808	769
Energy (fpe)	333	298	268	243
Deviation (in.; 100-yd. zero)	0	+ 5.6	0	− 18.8
Deviation (25-yd. zero)	0	− 2	− 15.2	− 41.7

.45 AUTO (230-GRAIN)

	Muzzle	50 yds.	100 yds.	150 yds.
Velocity (fps)	800	774	750	727
Energy (fpe)	327	306	287	270
Deviation (in.)	0	+ 6.8	0	− 22.2
Deviation (25-yd. zero)	0	− 2.7	− 19.1	− 50.9

.45 WINCHESTER MAGNUM (230-GRAIN)
5½-INCH BARREL

	Muzzle	50 yds.	100 yds.	150 yds.
Velocity (fps)	1400	1277	1176	1100
Energy (fpe)	1001	833	706	618
Deviation (in.)	0	+ 2.3	0	− 8.5
Deviation (25-yd. zero)	0	− 0.4	− 5.4	− 16.6

Appendix II

Manufacturers

American Derringer Corp.
127 Lacy Dr.
Waco, TX 76705
(.25 semiauto pistol)

AMT (Arcadia Machine & Tool)
536 N. Vincent Ave.
Covina, CA 91722
(AMT Hardballer, AMT Lightning, AMT Backup)

Arminex, Ltd.
7882 E. Gray Rd.
Scottsdale Airpark
Scottsdale, AZ 85260
(Makers of the Trifire Auto Pistol and accessories
   for it and other 1911-A1 style pistols)

Auto Nine Corp.
12521 Oxnard St.
North Hollywood, CA 91606
(Auto Nine Pistol)

Auto-Ordnance Corp.
Box ZG
West Hurley, NY 12491
(Manufacturer of the Auto-Ordnance 1911-A1)

Beretta USA
17601 Indian Head Highway
Accokeek, MD 20607
(Manufacturer and distributor of Beretta pistols)

Bersa
Attn: Publicity/Advertising Manager
P.O. Box 1327
Dayton, OH 45401

Browning
Rt. 1
Morgan, UT 84050
(Distributor for the Browning Double-Action
   9mm, Browning Hi-Power, Challenger III, and
   Buck Mark .22)

Caspian Arms, Ltd.
Hardwick, VT 05843
(Manufacturers of a 1911-A1 copy)

Charter Arms
430 Sniffens Lane
Stratford, CT 06497
(Distributor of the 79K, 40 autos; manufacturer
  of the Explorer II)

Colt Industries
Firearms Division
P.O. Box 1868
Hartford, CT 06101
(Manufacturer of the Colt .45 ACP and .380 ACP
  automatics)

Coonan Arms, Inc.
830 Hampden Ave.
St. Paul, MN 55114

Detonics Mfg. Corp.
13456 S.E. 27th Pl.
Bellevue, WA 98005
(Manufacturer of the Pocket 9 auto and 1911-A1
  style pistol and accessories)

Dornaus & Dixon Enterprises
15896 Manufacture Lane
Huntington Beach, CA 92649
(Manufacturer of the Bren Ten)

Excam Inc.
4480 E. 11 Ave.
P.O. Box 3483
Hialeah, FL 33013
(Importer of TZ-90 semiauto)

F.I.E. (Firearms Importers and Exporting Corp.)
P.O. Box 4866
Hialeah Lakes
Hialeah, FL 33014
(Importer of Titan pistol and various TZ-75
  models)

Fraser Firearms Corp.
34575 Commerce
Fraser, MI 48026
(Fraser .25 semiauto)

Glock, Inc.
P.O. Box 369
Smyrna, GA 30081
(Importer of the Glock pistol)

Gun South, Inc.
P.O. Box 6607
Birmingham, AL 35210
(Distributor of Steyr GB 9mm semiauto)

Heckler & Koch
14601 Lee Rd.
Chantilly, VA 22021
(Manufacturer/distributor of P-7, VP-70, etc.)

Interarms
10 Prince St.
Alexandria, VA 22313
(Importer of SIG, Walther, and Astra pistols)

Iver Johnson
2202 Redmond Rd.
Jacksonville, AR 72076
(Manufacturer of P0380 Pony, Trailsman, and
  9mm auto pistols)

Jennings Firearms
4510 Carter Ct.
Chino, CA 91710
(Manufacturer of the J-22 .22 LR auto pistol)

Kassnar Imports
5480 Linglestown Rd.
Harrisburg, PA 17110
(Concorde PMK 380 and MBK-9HP auto pistols)

L.A.R. Manufacturing, Inc.
4133 West Farm Rd.
West Jordan, UT 84084
(Makers of L.A.R. Grizzly auto pistol)

L.W. Seecamp Company
P.O. Box 255
New Haven, CT 06502
(Maker of LWS-25 and LWS-32 auto pistols)

Magnum Research, Inc.
Attn: Douglas A. Evans
7271 Commerce Circle West
Minneapolis, MN 55432
(Desert Eagle .357/.44 Magnum Autos)

Daisy Air Rifles' Model 09 "soft air" gun is a carefully made model of the Beretta 92-F. The Daisy gun fires small plastic pellets. Ideal for training new shooters to handle the pistol safely, it has a limited use for safely practicing quick draws and instinctive shooting in areas where a real firearm can't be safely used. Photo courtesy of Daisy Manufacturing Corp.

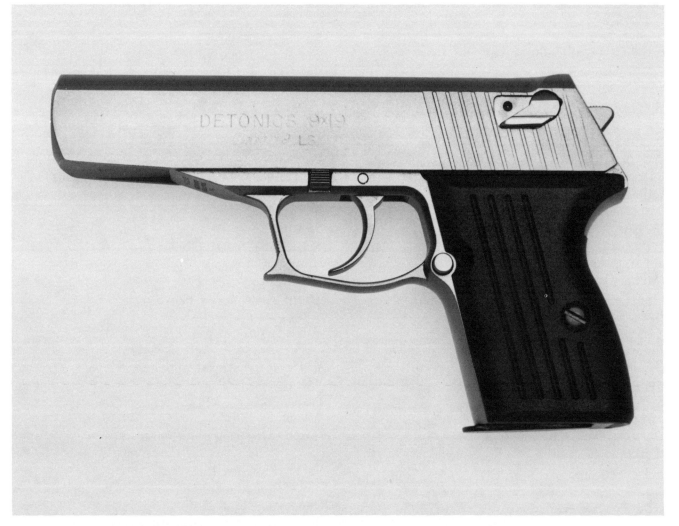

The Detonics Pocket 9LS has a slide-mounted ambidextrous thumb safety/firing pin block and a double-action trigger. The sights are grooved into the top of the slide to keep them snagfree when the pistol is carried concealed in clothing. The standard "Pocket 9" has a slightly shorter barrel than this version. Photo courtesy of Detonics.

Mandall Shooting Supplies
3616 N. Scottsdale Rd.
Scottsdale, AZ 85252
(Turkish MKE auto pistol)

Matra-Manurhin International
631 S. Washington St.
Alexandria, VA 22314
(Importer of Manurhin-made Walther PP and
    PPK/S auto pistols)

O.D.I., Inc.
124 A Greenwood Ave.
Midland Park, NJ 07432
(9mm and .45 ACP Viking Combat D.A. pistols)

Osborne's Shooting Supplies
P.O. Box 408
Cheboygan, MI 49721
(Importer of SIG, Korth, CZ-75, and Walther
    pistols)

Outdoor Sports Headquarters
967 Watertower Ln.
Dayton, OH 45449
(Importer of Bersa semiauto pistols)

Pacific International Merchandising Corp.
P.O. Box 8022
Sacramento, CA 95818
(Military/police surplus firearms)

Paragon Sales & Services, Inc.
P.O. Box 2022
Joliet, IL 60434
(Military surplus firearms)

Raven Arms
1300 Bixby Dr.
Industry, CA 91745
(Manufacturers of the Raven MP-25 pistol)

SGW
624 Old Pacific Hwy. S.E.
Olympia, WA 98503
(Parts and accessories for .45 Auto and other
    pistols)

Sherman Compensator Systems
2474 Highway 50 East
Carson City, NV 89701
(MP Express Gun and Sherman II compensator for
    .45 auto pistol)

Sigarms, Inc.
8330 Old Courthouse Rd., Suite 885
Tysons Corner, VA 22180
(Importer of SIG-Sauer auto pistols)

Sile Distributors
7 Centre Market Pl.
New York, NY 10013
(Importer of Benelli auto pistols)

Smith & Wesson, Inc.
2100 Roosevelt Ave.
Springfield, MA 01101
(Manufacturer of 439/469/459, etc. auto pistols)

Springfield Armory
111 E. Exchange St.
Geneseo, IL 61254
(Manufacturer of 1911-A1 style auto)

Steel City Arms
1883 Main St.
Pittsburgh, PA 15215
(War Eagle 9mm auto, Double Deuce pistol)

Stoeger Industries
55 Ruta Ct.
S. Hackensack, NJ 07606
(Importer of Llama pistols)

Sturm, Ruger & Company
Southport, CT 06490
(Manufacturer of Ruger Mark I & II)

Taurus International Mfg., Inc.
P.O. Box 558567
Ludlam Br.
Miami, FL 33155
(Importer of Taurus auto pistols)

Wildey Firearms, Inc.
299 Washington St.
Newburgh, NY 12550
(Manufacturer of Wildey Auto-Mag pistols)

Wilkerson Firearms Corp.
P.O. Box 157
Westminster, CA 92684
(Manufacturer of American Arms Eagle 380 auto)

Wilkinson Arms
26884 Pearl Rd.
Parma, ID 83660
(Manufacturer of Sherry .22 auto pistol)

ACCESSORIES

Ace Case Company
1530 Pheasant Ridge
Ellisville, MO 63011
(Leather pistol cases)

Alessi
2465 Niagara Falls Blvd.
Tonawanda, NY 14150
(Leather concealment holsters)

Armson
P.O. Box 2130
Farmington Hills, MI 48018
(Armson O.E.G. available-light dot scope and
   Trijicon sight inserts for pistols)

Assault Systems
869 Horan Dr.
St. Louis, MO 63026
(Pistol cases and accessories)

Beeman Precision Arms
47 Paul Dr.
San Rafael, CA 94903
(Maker of air pistols suitable for practice)

Brigade Quartermasters, Ltd.
266 Roswell St.
Marietta, GA 30060-9988
(Holsters, pistol pouches, accessories, etc.)

Brownells, Inc.
Rt. 2, Box 1
Montezuma, IA 50171
(Distributor for a wide range of firearms acces-
   sories, reloading and gunsmithing equipment.
   Sells the Clark "45" pistol grip for the Ruger
   Mark I/II, Pachmayr products, and a wealth
   of other equipment.)

James E. Clark, Pistolsmith
Rt. 2, Box 22A
Keithville, LA 71047
(Maker of scope mounts for 1911-A1 pistols)

Daisy Manufacturing Company, Inc.
P.O. Box 220
Rogers, AR 72757
(Sells a number of "Softair" pistols which might be
   considered for training or practice. Their 92
   Powerline is the CO2 version of the Beretta 92;
   it is excellent for developing instinctive shooting
   skills without a large expenditure of money.)

E&L Manufacturing, Inc.
Star Rt. 2, Box 569
Schoolhouse Rd.
Cave Creek, AZ 85331
(Maker of the "Rigid Brass Catcher" for the
   1911-A1)

Eaton Supply, Inc.
5340 E. Hunter Ave.
Anaheim, CA 92807
(Maker of standard size and extended magazines
   for the 1911-A1, AMT, Browning Hi-Power, and
   Walther PPK, PPK/S)

Jonathan Arthur Ciener
R.D. 2, Box 66Y6
Titusville, FL 32780
(Manufacturer of silencers for semiauto pistols)

Julio Santiago
P.O. Box O
Rosemount, MN 55068
(Santiago sells excellent rapid-fire targets for
   developing skills in day or night instinctive fire.
   In addition, Julio Santiago is available to do
   consultation work and seminars for police
   personnel.)

In addition to their holster line, Michaels of Oregon makes good magazine pouches which hold the magazines firmly but allow them to be retrieved in a hurry. The pouches are available in most gun stores. Photo courtesy of Michaels of Oregon.

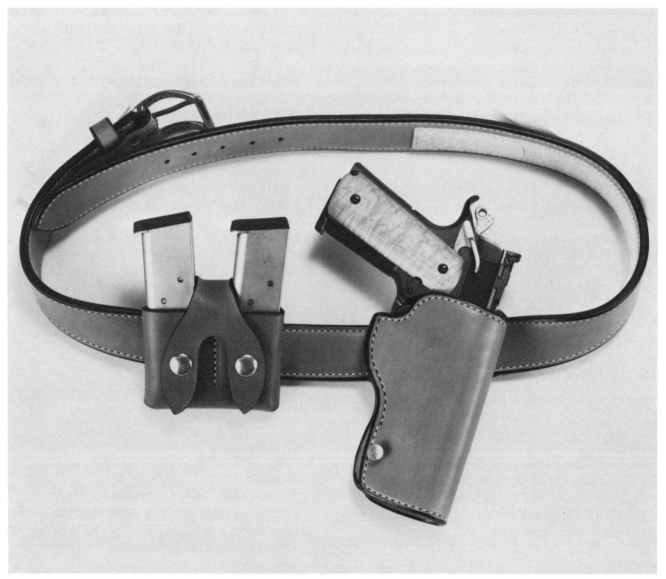

A good holster and magazine carriers are essential. Milt Sparks offers a number of excellent leather holsters and accessories for owners of any of the 1911-A1-style pistols. Photo courtesy of Milt Sparks.

Mag-Na-Port
41302 Executive Dr.
Mount Clemens, MI 48045-3448
(This company will cut gas ports in the barrels of
  firearms. This work will reduce muzzle jump and
  is especially useful on magnum pistols.)

Michaels of Oregon Company
P.O. Box 13010
Portland, OR 97213
(Maker of the excellent "Uncle Mike's" nylon
  holsters, belts, and belt pouches for a wide
  variety of pistols)

Milt Sparks
P.O. Box 187
Idaho City, ID 83631
(Maker of excellent concealment holsters)

Newman's GI Supply
RR #1, Box 782
Augusta, NJ 07822
(Combat support vests, military surplus gear)

Pachmayr
1220 South Grand Ave.
P.O. Box 15053
Los Angeles, CA 90015
(Rubber recoil-absorbing grips for most revolvers
  and auto pistols, and accessory parts for 1911-
  A1, Browning Hi-Power, and Dominator
  conversion kit for 1911-A1 pistols)

Parellex Corporation
1090 Fargo
Elk Grove, IL 60007
(Distributor of magazines, gun cases, etc.)

Ram Line
406 Violet St.
Golden, CO 80401
(New 12-round magazines for Ruger Mark I/II,
  Mark I/II magazine quick release, 25-round
  Explorer II magazine)

Red-E Products, Inc.
2101 E. Beverly
Tucson, AZ 85719
(Maker of "One Hand Magazine Release," for
  Ruger Mark I/II)

Security Operations Consultants, Inc.
18430 Brookhurst #205
Fountain Valley, CA 92708
(Model XR/400 laser-aiming system for pistols)

Sierra Supply
P.O. Box 1390
Durango, CO 81301
(Break-Free Lubricants, military surplus gear, U.S.
  Army Beretta Pistol Manual)

SGW
624 Old Pacific Highway, SE
Olympia, WA 98503
(Colt .45 accessories and new and military surplus
  parts)

Sherwood International
18714 Parthenia St.
Northridge, CA 91324
(Magazines, gun cases, .45 auto parts, etc.)

Triple K Manufacturing Company
568 Sixth Ave.
San Diego, CA 92101
(Manufacturer of wide number of magazines for
  various firearms)

Appendix III

Publications and Video Tapes

The following books and magazines have valuable information about various pistols, accessories, and handgun developments.

American Rifleman
1600 Rhode Island Ave., NW
Washington, DC 20036
   This magazine gives realistic reviews of pistols as well as excellent articles of historic interest.

The Browning Hi-Power Exotic Weapons System
Paladin Press
P.O. Box 1307
Boulder, CO 80306
   Two ways to convert the Hi-Power to selective fire are given in this book, as well as detailed plans for creating a forward grip to help control the pistol during automatic fire.

Combat Ammunition
Duncan Long
Paladin Press
P.O. Box 1307
Boulder, CO 80306

This book covers both commercial ammunition as well as how to modify it or reload your own ammunition for combat.

Combat Arms
Petersen Publishing Company
8490 Sunset Blvd.
Los Angeles, CA 90069
   While this magazine is aimed at large equipment and the high-tech end of combat, it also has interesting reviews of newer small arms.

Combat Handguns
Harris Publications
1115 Broadway
NY, NY 10010
   This is *the* magazine that covers new pistols, accessories, tactics, etc. It has good ideas and is realistic about what happens in—and is needed for—combat with handguns.

Combat Weapons
P.O. Box 401
Mt. Morris, IL 61054

Although this magazine is aimed at large equipment and grand strategies and high-tech equipment, it also has interesting reviews of newer small arms and lets readers know what's being produced in other countries.

Consumer's Guide to Handguns
Aaron S. Zelman and Lt. Michael L. Neuens
Stackpole Books
P.O. Box 1831
Harrisburg, PA 17105
This book tests out a few of the more common combat pistols with some surprising results.

Deadly Weapons tape
Deadly Weapons
P.O. Box 375
Pinole, CA 94564
Hands-on tests and information about how effective pistol bullets really are and what they can—and can't—do are shown in this tape available in VHS or Beta.

Firepower
P.O. Box 397
Cornville, AZ 86325
While the staff seems enamored with the .45 ACP, the magazine does give tough reviews of firearms and isn't afraid to point out the faults of many guns.

Gun Digest
Edited by Ken Warner
DBI Books
4092 Commercial Ave.
Northbrook, IL 60062
This annual is a treasury of information about new firearms as well as interesting historical articles.

Master Tips
Jon Winokur
P.O. Box 1117
Pacific Palisades, CA 90272-1117
Aimed at combat pistol contest shooters, this book has interviews with great U.S. shooters who give their secrets of holding, aiming, etc.

The basics of safety and gun handling are also covered and make this book a valuable addition to your library.

New Breed
Box 428
Nanuet, NY 10954
Although this magazine seems to dwell on the Vietnam War, it also has good articles from time to time about small arms.

Principles of Personal Defense
Jeff Cooper
Paladin Press
P.O. Box 1307
Boulder, CO 80306
Though Cooper's ideas about the ideal caliber are a bit outdated, this classic book gives excellent and realistic information on using a handgun in combat.

Silencers in the 1980s
J. David Truby
Paladin Press
P.O. Box 1307
Boulder, CO 80306
A good overall look at the various styles of suppressors available is given in this book.

Small Arms of the World
Edward Clinton Ezell
Stackpole Books
P.O. Box 1831
Harrisburg, PA 17105
In addition to covering machine guns and military rifles, this book gives some excellent information, along with interesting photos, of pistols currently in use throughout the world.

Soldier of Fortune
P.O. Box 348
Mt. Morris, IL 61054
Devoted mostly to military combat articles, this magazine also has well-written and interesting reviews of both new and old pistols and other small arms.

Appendix IV

Troubleshooting

A combat weapon must function perfectly when you need it. Failure to do so can prove fatal. Combat weapons are expected to work under conditions and for time periods that would destroy a sporting weapon.

An important step to take with any firearm is to read the owner's manual. Many times a pistol will have quirks which make it easily damaged during disassembly or cleaning, or with some types of ammunition. If you purchase a current production handgun and it doesn't have a manual, the manufacturer will be happy to send you a free one.

A large percentage of pistol malfunctions can be directly traced to poor ammunition. Ammunition can be damaged by oil, bore cleaner, or water; great care must be taken to protect cartridges from weather or weapon lubricant. Heat also lowers ammunition performance. If you keep a pistol in a car that becomes excessively hot, ammunition should be periodically replaced.

It is important to break in your handgun. Firearms come from the manufacturer with some rough edges that quickly wear down after several hundred rounds. A firearm will often custom fit its parts and function very reliably.

One practice that seems to be hard on pistols is dry firing. This tends to weaken firing pins and may peen other parts. Practice with live ammunition if possible or purchase practice ammunition designed to protect the firing pin when dry firing. Avoid "hot" ammunition. Few firearms can fire hot loads without eventually shaking loose; save such loads for combat or *occasional* practice.

It is wise to have a gunsmith smooth out the feed ramp and throat the barrel so that the weapon can digest a wide range of ammunition. You can never tell what you may be forced to use. Having a firearm that will only work reliably with FMJ ammunition or the like is a handicap that could prove disastrous.

Keep your handgun clean. In addition to aiding reliability, you can prevent a lot of the wear created by small amounts of grit. A clean pistol lasts longer and is less apt to fail than an identical, but dirty, firearm. Improper cleaning can ruin a gun's accuracy; when possible, clean from the chamber end and avoid letting the cleaning rod touch or rub against the muzzle. The exact size and smoothness of the last fraction of an inch of the barrel will often determine the accuracy of the gun.

Avoid over-lubricating; this attracts dirt. Replace parts when they show signs of excessive wear. A spare firing pin and various springs are wise to have with either a revolver or automatic. An extractor and other small parts are also wise purchases.

Keep modifications to a minimum. Don't try any do-it-yourself modifications or gunsmith work unless you really know what you're doing. A lot of damage can be done with kitchen-table gunsmithing. If it's not broken, don't fix it.

While automatics are often more reliable than revolvers, they do fail from time to time. There are some quick steps you should go through to be sure that some simple thing hasn't caused a failure.

1. If you have a double-action pistol, pull on the trigger; often a bad primer will fire when hit a second time.

2. Tap the magazine to be sure it's seated and recycle the slide. This will ensure that a new round is in the chamber if a faulty one was there first. If the slide doesn't go all the way into the locked position, tap it shut before trying to fire.

3. If the weapon doesn't fire, replace the magazine, cycle the slide, and try to fire again.

4. If the slide fails to go clear forward so that a round can be fired, remove the magazine, place the safety into the on position, and lock the slide open. There may be an obstruction in the chamber or slide face. Examine them carefully and remove the obstacle. Then reseat the magazine, reload, disengage the safety, and fire.

5. If you have a stovepipe jam (an empty cartridge in the ejection port), pull back slightly on the slide while tilting the port downward so the jammed cartridge is removed, or brush the brass out of the port by stroking your hand down the top of the slide. If the gun fails to fire, chamber another round and try again.

6. If the trigger fails to release the hammer, check the safety to be sure it is in the fire position. Check other safety features, such as magazine safety, which may be built into the handgun.

No matter how careful you are in keeping your pistol clean and well maintained, your weapon will probably fail some time. Knowing how to get it functioning quickly can mean the difference between life and death. Read and study the procedures below so you know what to do.

Some of these procedures are dangerous and should only be engaged in when your life is on the line; don't attempt the actual measures with live ammunition unless not having a weapon is more dangerous than possible injury. The best way to get a firearm fixed is to take it to a gunsmith!

There are many differences in parts and operation among the various types, brands, and models of pistols; therefore some of the following steps will not apply to your own weapon.

AUTOMATIC PISTOL TROUBLESHOOTING PROCEDURES

PROBLEM	CHECK FOR	REPAIR PROCEDURE
1. Firearm won't cock; safety doesn't work properly.	Worn, broken, or missing parts.	Check parts and replace.
2. Firearm continues to fire after the trigger is released.	Dirt in trigger/sear mechanism.	Clean.
	Broken sear/trigger.	Replace sear/trigger.
	Weak sear/trigger spring.	Replace spring.
	Bent or peened firing pin.	Replace firing pin.
	Weak ammunition (blowback weapons only).	Replace ammunition.

PROBLEM	CHECK FOR	REPAIR PROCEDURE
3. Firearm won't fire.	Safety on Safe.	Place in fire position.
	Firing pin missing or broken.	Replace firing pin.
	Too much oil or dirt in firing pin recess.	Wipe/clean.
	Poor ammo.	Remove/discard.
	Internal parts are defective/worn or broken.	Remove, clean, and/or replace.
	Weak or broken hammer, striker, or sear spring.	Replace.
	Bolt not locking.	Clean dirty parts.
	Firing pin block or other safety is broken.	Repair.
4. Round won't chamber.	Dirty or corroded ammo.	Clean ammo.
	Damaged ammo.	Replace.
	Fouling in chamber.	Clean with chamber brush.
	Broken or damaged recoil spring.	Repair or replace.
5. Rounds won't eject.	Broken ejector.	Replace.
	Frozen ejector.	Clean/lubricate.
	Bad ejector spring.	Replace.
6. Rounds won't extract.	Broken extractor.	Replace.
	Dirty/corroded ammo.	Remove (may have to be carefully pushed out with cleaning rod).
	Carbon/fouling in chamber or extractor lip.	Clean chamber and lip.
	Broken extractor or bad spring.	Replace.
	Dirty/faulty recoil spring.	Clean/replace.
	Dirty or pitted chamber.	Clean or replace.

PROBLEM	CHECK FOR	REPAIR PROCEDURE
7. Rounds won't feed.	Dirty or corroded ammo.	Clean ammo.
	Low-powered ammo.	Use different ammo.
	Defective magazine.	Replace magazine.
	Dirt in magazine.	Clean and lubricate magazine.
	Too many rounds in magazine.	Remove several rounds.
	Magazine not seated.	Reseat magazine.
	Broken magazine catch.	Repair/replace.
	Improperly assembled or broken magazine.	Reassemble or replace.
8. Safety lever binds.	Fouling/lack of lubrication.	Lubricate; if lever still binds, disassemble and clean.
9. Safety/hammer drop does not lower hammer.	Broken mechanism.	Repair.
10. Slide does not hold open after last round (if weapon has hold-open device).	Fouled/broken slide latch.	Clean/replace.
	Bad magazine.	Discard magazine.
11. Slide doesn't fully close into battery.	Round jammed in chamber.	*Danger: Stay clear of the muzzle.* Remove the magazine and cycle slide to remove cartridge. If this fails, try using cleaning rod to remove the cartridge.
	Extractor frozen in down position.	Remove and clean extractor.
	Recoil spring not moving freely.	Remove, clean, and lubricate.
	Recoil spring broken or bent.	Repair or replace.
	Recoil spring rod bent.	Check and replace or straighten rod.
	Dirt in locking lugs.	Clean.
	Lack of lubrication.	Relubricate.

PROBLEM	CHECK FOR	REPAIR PROCEDURE
	Dirty or burred slide rails.	Clean or repair.
	Damaged locking block or lugs.	Repair.
12. Slide won't cycle.	Dirty or burred slide rails.	Clean or repair.
	Cartridge jammed in chamber.	*Danger: Stay clear of muzzle.* Remove the magazine and cycle slide to remove cartridge. If this fails, try using cleaning rod to remove the cartridge.
	Broken or damaged locking block or lugs.	Repair.
	Broken slide.	Replace.

Appendix V

The U.S. Armed Forces Pistol Choice

The decision to adopt a 9mm pistol as standard issue of the U.S. Armed Forces didn't occur overnight. The U.S. military had toyed with the idea in 1949 but dropped it, since a large number of new 1911-A1 .45 ACP pistols had already been purchased in 1945.

The U.S. Air Force was never enamored with the .45 and, following World War II, began to purchase a number of different pistols—mostly .38 revolvers—for air crews. In 1976, the Air Force conducted its own tests of commercial 9mm automatics. A year later, perhaps taking the lead from the Air Force, the Department of Defense tried to get money for development of a brand-new .38-caliber handgun cartridge.

The Air Force tests proved inconclusive, and the other branches of the military jumped into the work to choose a new pistol and/or caliber. In 1978 the Department of Defense stepped in to set up the Joint Services Small Arms Program (JSSAP), which was to select a pistol to be used by all branches of the miltiary. (The JSSAP probably saved the taxpayers a lot of money by eliminating duplicated research, thereby speeding up the selection process on the part of the military.)

In 1980, the JSSAP recommended that a 9mm Luger handgun be adopted in several versions, one standard-sized weapon and a smaller one which could be concealed for special use. Several tests were conducted with 40 guns submitted by Beretta, Browning (FN), Colt, H&K, S&W, SIG, Steyr, and Walther.

Colt's entry into the test consisted of a standard 1911-A1 in 9mm. Colt's argument was that 1911-A1s in stock could be retrofitted to be used as 9mm pistols and training, manuals, etc., could remain the same. However, the 1911-A1 pistols in the U.S. armory were all but worn out, and the new guns had a very limited magazine capacity. The race was thrown open to all manufacturers to develop a new side arm for the U.S. soldier.

After some false starts (and threats of lawsuits by the losers of the contest for acceptance), two pistols made it through the maze of requirements and stringent tests. They were the SIG pistol and the Beretta 92SB-F.

Beretta had set the stage for winning the contract long before the tests were finalized. Following the 1968 gun laws that had restricted the importation of small guns into the U.S., Beretta had slowly purchased assembly and manufacturing plants in the States in order to get in on the lucrative U.S. civilian market. As a result, Beretta was well on its way toward setting up operations to build the Series 92 pistols in the U.S. when the military test requirements were set up. The requirements specified that the company which won the government contract would have to build the pistols in the U.S.

Thus, when the choice had to be made between the SIG-Sauer pistol and Beretta, Beretta was able to give a lower bid on its pistols. Money being tight and the two different pistols being equally suitable, the U.S. military announced Beretta the winner of the contract on January 14, 1985. The five-year procurement package called for 315,930 pistols to be purchased for slightly over 56 million dollars. Pistols for the first year would come from Italy with the Beretta's U.S. plant gradually taking over the manufacture of the pistols.

At the time of this writing, the fate of the U.S. military's M9 pistol—the Beretta 92-F—is up in the air. A report from the General Accounting Office was critical of the procurement process used to select the Beretta pistol, and other companies that were contenders in the military tests have been disgruntled as well. These two pressures led to the June 5, 1986, meeting of the Legislation and Security Subcommittee of the House Government Operations Committee. The Subcommittee recommended that the Beretta contract with the U.S. Army be canceled after the current order is filled and that yet another competition be held to select a pistol to fulfill the remaining pistol orders of the service.

It is probable that *if* another round of tests for a new standard pistol takes place, Beretta will again come out on top. If it doesn't, the U.S. military will again have several different pistols in its inventory which will complicate supply and repair problems—one of the very problems the selection of a standard pistol was designed to eliminate in the first place.